Between men and feminism

Between Men and Feminism had its origins in a lively colloquium at St John's College, Cambridge in 1990. It discusses how two decades of feminism have affected the ways men define their own masculinities, and how they have responded in their social, sexual and political lives to the challenges posed by the evolving feminist critiques of patriarchy and maleness itself.

The collection contains a great diversity of approaches and perspectives from Britain and North America. It includes viewpoints from academics, a poet, an educational researcher, and the members of an active men's group. Gay issues feature prominently, as do psychoanalytical views, and a number of the pieces provide a refreshingly personal and practical outlook.

Between Men and Feminism shows men finding their own way within the spaces feminism has opened to them, rediscovering their own gendered voices and participating in the transformation of controlling ideologies in their daily lives. These very readable accounts will appeal not only to students in the social sciences and gender studies, but to all men who find themselves responding to the feminist challenge.

David Porter is in the Department of Comparative Literature at Stanford University.

Between men
and feminism

Edited by David Porter

London and New York

First published in 1992
by Routledge
11 New Fetter Lane, London EC4P 4EE

Simultaneously published in the USA and Canada
by Routledge
a division of Routledge, Chapman and Hall Inc.
29 West 35th Street, New York, NY 10001

© 1992 David Porter, the collection as a whole; individual chapters, the
contributors

Typeset in Palatino by LaserScript, Mitcham, Surrey
Printed and bound in Great Britain by Biddles Ltd, Guildford
and King's Lynn

British Library Cataloguing in Publication Data

A catalogue record for this book is available from the British Library.

Library of Congress Cataloging in Publication Data

Between men and feminism/edited by David Porter.
    p.
Includes bibliographical references and index.
1. Men.   2. Men – Psychology.   3. Sex role.   4. Feminism.
I. Porter, David, 1965–
HQ1090.B477   1993
305.3–dc20   92-10405
                                                                  CIP

ISBN 0–415–06987–4 (hbk)
ISBN 0–415–06988–2 (pbk)

For my parents

Contents

Contributors

Joseph A. Boone is an associate professor of English at the University of Southern California, and the author of *Tradition Counter Tradition: Love and the Form of Fiction* (1987), and co-editor, with Michael Cadden, of *Engendering Men: The Question of Male Feminist Criticism* (Routledge, 1990). He is currently at work on two longer projects, one on sexuality, narrative and modernity, and the other on the homoerotics of Orientalism in narratives of the Near East.

Gregory W. Bredbeck is associate professor of English at the University of California, Riverside, where he teaches courses in sixteenth- and seventeenth-century English literature, gay and lesbian modern and postmodern literature, and queer theory. He received his PhD from the University of Pennsylvania, and is the author of *Sodomy and Interpretation: Marlowe to Milton* (1991). He has published articles on both Renaissance and postmodern gay studies in *PMLA, The Journal of Homosexuality*, and several anthologies. The essay included here is part of a book-in-progress tentatively titled *Stone/Wall: Postmodern Economies of Gay Identity*.

Joseph Bristow is a lecturer in English literature at the University of York. He previously taught at Sheffield City Polytechnic. His books include *Empire Boys: Adventures in a Man's World* (1991) and *Robert Browning: New Readings* (1991). He has recently edited *Sexual Sameness: Textual Differences in Lesbian and Gay Writing* and *Oscar Wilde: The Importance of Being Earnest and Related Writings* (both Routledge, 1992).

The **Cambridge Men's Group** is a small circle of men in the Cambridge community who have met fortnightly since 1984 to discuss issues of gender and masculinity in their daily lives. The present essay is their first experiment in collaborative writing, but they have given group presentations, helped to set up other men's groups, and participated in national men's anti-sexism events in the UK.

John Forrester is a lecturer in history and philosophy of science at Cambridge University. He is the author of *Language and the Origins of Psychoanalysis* (1980), *The Seductions of Psychoanalysis: Freud, Lacan and Derrida* (1990) and, with Lisa Appignanesi, *Freud's Women* (1992).

Jeff Hearn is reader in sociology and critical studies on men, University of Bradford. He has been involved in men's groups and anti-sexist activities since 1978. He is the author of numerous articles; his books include *'Sex' at 'Work'* (co-author, 1987), *The Gender of Oppression* (1987), *The Sexuality of Organization* (co-editor, 1989), *Taking Child Abuse Seriously* (co-editor, 1990), and *Men, Masculinities, and Social Theory* (co-editor, 1990), and *Men in the Public Eye* (1992). He is series editor of Critical Studies on Men and Masculinities (Routledge) and co-convener of the Violence, Abuse, and Gender Relations Research Unit, University of Bradford.

Martin Humphries is poetry editor for GMP publishers. His books include *Mirrors* (1980), *Searching for a Destination* (1982) and *Salt in Honey* with Steve Cranfield (1989). He compiled and introduced *Not Love Alone* (1985), the first anthology of contemporary gay men's poetry to be published in England. He co-edited with Andy Metcalf *The Sexuality of Men* (1985) and *Heterosexuality* with Gillian Hanscombe (1987). He has organized Poetry for AIDS readings in London. With his lover, Ronald Grant, he founded The Cinema Museum in 1984 to develop and preserve a huge collection of cinema ephemera.

David Porter, a graduate of Cornell and Cambridge Universities, is currently a doctoral candidate in comparative literature at Stanford. He has written on Kafka's *The Trial* and on issues of sexuality and desire in medieval poetry, and was the founding editor of an alternative graduate student newspaper at Stanford. His current projects include work on narratives of exile, theory of multiculturalism, and a Chinese language word processor. He has published an astronomy program for personal computers called *SkyWatch*.

Naomi Segal is a Fellow of St John's College, Cambridge, where she teaches French and comparative literature. She has published many articles and is the co-editor of a book on Freud and author of four other books: *The Banal Object: Theme and Thematics in Proust, Rilke, Hofmannsthal and Sartre* (1981), *The Unintended Reader: Feminism and 'Manon Lescaut'* (1986), *Narcissus and Echo: Women in the French Récit* (1988) and *The Adulteress's Child* (forthcoming, 1992). She has a daughter and a son.

Andrea Spurling has worked as an independent research consultant in the area of graduate career development since 1980. In 1988 she was appointed to run the *Women in Higher Education Project* at King's College, Cambridge. This project identified factors inhibiting women's progress to senior academic levels at Cambridge University, and contributed to changes in policy and practice in the College and in the University. She is currently Head of Programmes at The Council for Industry and Higher Education in London, where she manages a research-based project on the use and development of science and engineering graduates in British industry. She is the author of several articles on institutional prejudice and education.

Acknowledgements

I would like to express my thanks to all the friends, teachers, and colleagues without whom this project would never have been possible. My first thanks go to the contributors themselves, whose forbearance and cooperation in dealing with a first-time editor were matched only by the thoughtfulness of their work in making the process a manageable and even enjoyable one. One of the contributors, Naomi Segal, helped to organize the original Men and Feminism Colloquium at Cambridge, and first encouraged me to publish the proceedings. Kate White assisted in planning the colloquium, and Isabel Holowaty contributed generously to the preparation of an initial abstract for the book. A special thanks goes to Robert Gordon and David Halpern, who for two years steered me patiently through the cultural labyrinths of the Cambridge scene, enabling me to come out with something to say at the other end.

At Stanford, the enthusiastic support of my advisors Hans Ulrich Gumbrecht and Herbert Lindenberger enabled me to integrate my work on the book into a full-time graduate program, and Patricia Parker provided much-needed encouragement and logistical advice in the final preparation of the manuscript. Karen Rezendes provided valuable administrative support, and Scott Mackey, in never-ending discussions, challenged me to keep the volume's feet on the ground, and to edit for the broader audience my title seemed to imply. I would also like to acknowledge Biddy Martin, whose excellent seminar on feminist theory got me thinking about these things at Cornell, and Jen Ruesink, who in this course and afterwards helped me work through their implications for my own life.

The colloquium was made possible through the generous support of the Department of French at Cambridge, the Master and Fellows of St John's College, and the trustees of the Judith E. Wilson Fund. Fellowships from the Keasbey Memorial Foundation and the Mellon Fellowship Program of the Woodrow Wilson Foundation have supported my research and writing during the two years this book has been in the making.

Finally, a very special thanks to Lan Wang, whose generosity, affection, and encouragement have made the book a source of new meanings and pleasures for me in the final stages of its preparation, and to my parents, who have given me the faith and courage to follow them in what they have done.

Introduction

David Porter

Cambridge University, for all its charms, has never been a particularly hospitable place for women. When Virginia Woolf arrived in 1928 to give the series of lectures that would later become *A Room of One's Own*, she was whisked away from a famous college library and served plain gravy soup for dinner, both on account of her sex. By the time Shere Hite appeared 62 years later to speak on her most recent research on women and love, the doors had opened and the food improved, but little beneath the surface had changed. The last all-male colleges had finally admitted women only two years previously, but few sectors of the university establishment were ready to accept the newcomers as full and equal members. In tutorials, rowing clubs, and even faculty meetings, women at Cambridge continued to meet with a potent mixture of resentment, condescension, and contempt.

Virginia Woolf responded with an appeal to women to claim for themselves a place from which to speak, a space within which to develop their voices as thinkers and writers, to cultivate that warm intellectual glow of the poets that circumstances and ideology had stifled for so long. When Shere Hite approached the podium at the Cambridge Union, she was ready to issue a different call. Though Cambridge as an institution resisted the fact, she spoke for a generation of women who had acquired, through feminism, new and powerful voices, and who had articulated thereby both thorough-going critiques of the culture of patriarchy and models for restructuring social relationships in every cultural sphere. Her talk that evening challenged men to come to grips with the on-going 'cultural revolution' she described, and to re-position themselves in relation to its new readings of love, gender, and sexuality.

There was nothing new, of course, in another invitation to men to reform their ways. But neither did the response Hite evoked from a male graduate student in the audience come as much of a surprise: 'I've heard so many times that men are the problem,' he said, 'that our fathers were the problem, that I am the problem now. I've been told I should change, rebuild my relationships from scratch, become a new, pro-feminist man. But frankly, these sorts of suggestions don't help me much, and neither does all the guilt. Maybe you can give me a straight answer. What is a man supposed to do?'

Her reply, however obvious in retrospect, was something of a revelation to me at the time, and gave rise, in a roundabout way, to the writing of this book. 'Talk to men,' she said. And in tones that made clear she'd given this reply many times before, she explained that although introspection and a commitment to personal change on the part of men were essential to the feminist project she envisioned, they would come to nothing without the simultaneous foundation of male communities of discourse dedicated to addressing these issues in a more public sphere, and conveying their urgency to that majority of men for whom feminism remained a negligible concern, or perhaps more commonly, an irritating thorn in the side.

The frustrated graduate student, it seemed to me, had spoken from within a chasm that Hite's hour at the lectern had opened somewhere beneath our feet. On the one hand, here was Cambridge, the Cambridge Union Society, no less, that paragon of elitist, male traditionalism where Members of Parliament and their natural successors sparred gamely over points of policy and the future of the Commonwealth. On the other was the voice of a woman who, however controversial her assumptions and her claims, seemed to speak at that moment for a solid and autonomous cultural formation that had taken shape somehow outside the Union's hallowed halls. The man's question had, for a moment, evoked the gulf between these two safe shores. Tentatively rejecting the first, but being a stranger to the second, he seemed to be groping, however cautiously, for a position between them to call his own.

Hite's suggestion would imply that any such space is primarily a discursive one, to be explored and mapped by men in talking to one another, reconstructing masculinity by coming to know it in all its forms, listening critically to its embodied voices and responding actively to what they hear. While such a project must inevitably draw on feminism for both its inspiration and its analytical tools, the nature of this relationship must be kept clear, in order to avoid gestures of appropriation of feminist space, or the temptation of self-vindication by association with it. Conversely, while men involved in such a dialogue will often strive to distance themselves from certain aspects of their own deeply gendered histories, the most compelling voices to emerge from this process will surely be those that engage directly with these histories in order to re-evaluate and potentially transform them.

The colloquium at St John's College for which most of the essays in this collection were first prepared grew out of my own desire to prompt an exploration of these discursive spaces in a setting where, as far as I could tell, the chasms were immense, and where among men, anyway, silence reigned. Hoping to bring as wide a range of perspectives to bear as possible on an elusive if provocative topic, I invited speakers from a number of fields within the university and a number of occupations outside it to present papers on topics of their choice under the rubric of 'Men and Feminism.' In the end, twelve took part in the six-week series in the spring of 1990.

Naomi Segal and John Forrester led off the colloquium with their papers on 'Why Can't a Good Man be Sexy? Why Can't a Sexy Man be Good?' and 'What Do Men Want?' to an audience that overflowed by a considerable margin the capacity of the modest meeting room we'd been assigned. The evident drawing power of the titles and the animated discussion that followed these and the subsequent presentations convinced me that there was in fact a space here that many others were anxious to explore. The primary concerns running through the series seemed to be how men, real, individual, embodied men – as opposed to the abstraction that feminism takes as its target in the popular imagination – had responded to the various interrogations of masculine identity that they had faced in the last twenty years, how women, in turn, viewed these responses (or the absence thereof), and how the masculinities represented in gay male culture illuminated both the violent agonies and the creative potentials of significant departures from dominant cultural norms.

Although the increasing currency of such questions among male academics can be glimpsed by paging through the bibliographies to some of the essays in this collection, for men to ask such questions in the spirit of personal self-reflection remains itself a bold departure from the comforting neutrality of abstraction or dismissal, and one that is still rarely undertaken. It is in the nature of any dominant cultural form – whether ideology, political institution, or academic discipline – to inhibit the sorts of enquiry into its own workings and origins that are likely to produce significant challenges to the stories by which it is maintained. To the extent that manhood, or patriarchy, or institutionalized sexism fits this category – and American manhood's seeming rejection of the very notion of sexual harassment in the recent Hill/Thomas hearings in Washington reminds us that they do – they are mum. The locker rooms are silent. And little surprise, at that, for what is there to say? When the distinctions between the normal and pathological varieties of 'masculinity' themselves begin to fade, as they did in this case, and as they do in sexual harassment and date rape cases across the country every day, there is little, as a man, to offer in one's defense.

But 'as a man' is, presumably, not the only position from which we (men) might speak. There is a great deal to be said, that must be said, but that can never be said from the rigid positions to which we confine ourselves out of fear or misplaced pride. I realized after the fact that the title of the original colloquium, 'Men and Feminism,' may have partially obscured the alternatives. The 'and' suggests a conjunction, a meeting place, a neatly closed relation that, I discovered, I was no closer to being able to formulate after the series than before. Men are as unlikely to articulate a juncture with feminism as they are a position inside it, and the attempt itself may well be just as problematic.[1] I am confident, however, that *between* the two poles a space does exist, and find that the relational nuances suggested by this modest preposition provide, at the very least, a compelling framework within which to read the provisional investigations that together comprise this volume.

To begin with, 'between' separates the terms that follow it, preventing confusion and mutual antagonism by establishing perhaps not boundaries so much as an unarticulated buffer zone. But if such a space brings with it possibilities for experimentation and change, it also evokes a very real fear of obscurity and silence, as the only voices to guide us here, the only models to follow will be our own. 'Between' connotes, in addition, the space of intimacy, of dialogue, of the potentially fruitful sharing of inspiration and example. If pro-feminist men don't belong *in* feminism *per se*, neither are they banished beyond its pale, and their debt to the struggles and critical agenda of their sisters is apparent in each one of their essays here.[2] But 'between' is also, in some cases, the site of barriers to such exchange. Whether theoretical objections to the implications of French feminist theory for gay men, or personal ambivalences on the part of women about just how far they want their men to change, conflict proves as vital in the emerging definitions of these spaces as mutuality and syncretism. Finally, I think that admitting a space between men and feminism destabilizes in a helpful way the static structure of the opposition itself. Though it may well be true, as one of the contributors claims, that the essential problem of feminism was and remains men, the terms of the antagonism are in constant flux as feminisms themselves divide and evolve, and the bearers of masculinity become increasingly cognizant of its margins. To insist on rigid dichotomies is to deny the import of these changes, and to thwart the liberatory impulse from which they stem.

It is in keeping, perhaps, with the openness of the topic that the contributors, as a group, cannot be easily pigeonholed. Of the seven colloquium participants and two additional writers who submitted essays for this volume, three are from outside the academy, two are women, and two concern themselves primarily with gay masculinities.[3] Both British and Californian viewpoints are represented, as are theoretical, political, pedagogical, poetic, and candid personal accounts of the writers' confrontations with the paradoxes of modern manhood. The style and length of the pieces vary considerably as well, frustrating any attempt, I should think, to read the collection as an inherently unified whole, but in this I see no need for apologies. Rather, I would venture to hope that the uncommon diversity of outspoken voices brought together here will count among the book's strengths: the uniformity that characterizes so much scholarship within established disciplines seems ill-suited to a project premised on the rejection of traditional institutional bases, and one whose success depends so substantially on the inclusion of a broadly heterogeneous community of men.

Diversity need not preclude organization, however, and bearing the above qualifications in mind I have grouped the nine essays according to phases of the overall project to which they seem to correspond. In the first section, 'Making space,' three essays present three very different preliminary mappings or articulations of the deeply variegated spaces between the institutions of manhood and the feminist challenges – personal, political, and theoretical – within which the ongoing analysis and transformation of masculinities continually arise.

For Joseph Boone, in the opening chapter, these spaces are already scarred by feminist apprehensions and the blindness of critical vogue. He challenges his fellow male critics to personalize the search for suitable places from which to speak their interest in and relation to feminism, in order to avoid bunching on bandwagons or becoming a parasite to someone else's cause. Whether the term 'men' actually belongs 'in,' 'and,' or 'after' feminism is ultimately less important, he argues, than how it is constituted by the multiplicity of 'me's' that it contains. The male critic's voice inhabits a body that reminds us constantly that his relation to feminism must be lived as well as theorized, and that the nature of this lived relation, rather than the critic's prominence within his field, is likely to determine the ultimate value of his contribution.

Naomi Segal views the interceding spaces as inscribed deeply with the politics of feminist heterosexual desire. An essential question for feminist women involved in relationships with men, she notes, is how their ideological expectations of their partners may affect their enjoyment of non-ideological pleasures. Can the 'good' man that a woman might want as a political ally, in other words, also be the 'sexy' man that she desires? In order to grapple more directly with the issue, Segal provides a provocative reading, informed by psychoanalysis, of five politically implicated components of a straight woman's experience of desire, and of those aspects of masculinity that are its object. What emerges from the series of bold and wide-ranging questions that structures the essay is a pronounced ambivalence towards the implications of certain kinds of feminist partnership on child-rearing, motherhood, and the pleasures – and politics – of intimacy.

Andrea Spurling turns the discussion from the unfamiliar spaces of hypothetical masculinities to the all too familiar dialogical spaces of the coeducational classroom. Based on research she conducted on the tutorial system at King's College, Cambridge, her essay develops the notion of silent spaces as an essential pedagogical tool, and describes how the differing perceptions and uses of such space between men and women determines the dynamic of the learning environment as a whole. She found not only that men tended to dominate discussions, but also that their discursive style was often viewed as aggressively intrusive by their women counterparts, and detracted from the learning process for both groups. Spurling proposes a cooperative discussion format, with a stress on group-oriented inquiry and the management of silence, as an alternative to the competitive norm.

The second section, 'Writing between the lines,' is concerned specifically with the project of (re)inscribing maleness within the spaces feminism has opened to it. These writings between the lines of a structural opposition follow directly from the corresponding mode of reading, and each of the essays in this section draws upon penetrating and unorthodox readings – whether literary, historical, or psychoanalytic – of contemporary constructions of masculine identities in its own representations.

For Joseph Bristow, the last twenty years have seen a dispersal of the concentration of critical energies in feminism represented by the publication of Kate Millett's *Sexual Politics*. What little common ground remains is frequently torn by high-handed theoretical polemics and name-calling, a situation often exacerbated by the generation of 'radical' straight male critics that has sprung up in the book's wake. The most pressing issues for men in sexual politics today will not be addressed in these turf wars, Bristow maintains, but through extensive re-readings and re-writings of personal and collective histories of men's experiences, and the building of recognition and alliances across the whole of the homosocial continuum. Like Andrea Spurling in the previous chapter, Bristow stresses the importance of the college classroom in promoting men's critical self-awareness, and he closes with practical suggestions on how the project he has outlined might be incorporated into an English curriculum.

The body, and specifically the male homosexual body, comes to the fore in Greg Bredbeck's incisive analysis of the politics of representation. Taking the notion of *écriture féminine* in the work of French feminists Cixous and Irigaray as his starting point, he demonstrates how even such potentially revolutionary re-writings of traditionally masculine poetics blindly re-inscribe the domination of the heterosexually coded body. If *écriture féminine* represses the homosexual impulse by replicating the discursive forms through which heterosexuality is sustained, gay male writing must seek a space of representation marked by differences to such semiotic hierarchies, rather than simply within them. Bredbeck offers a reading of Larry Kramer's *Faggots* to suggest how such a space might be constituted by reinstating the body, as he says, in the scene of writing as the author of its own desire.

Representing forms of male desire is also a central issue for John Forrester in the final essay in this section, but he approaches it here through a novel adaptation of a more familiar Freudian framework. Offering a twist on the traditional formulation, Forrester poses the question, 'What do men want?' and goes on to apply Freud's thinking on hysteria and the Dora case to an analysis of men's characteristic obsession with both power and sexual deviance. Combining an interpretation of the perversions as a form of defense against an all-powerful mother-figure with the observation of their nearly exclusive occurrence among men, he develops the challenging, if disturbing hypothesis that from a psychoanalytic standpoint, anyway, perversion may represent the purest expression of masculine sexuality.

The third and final section, entitled 'Between men: finding their own way,' might be read as a series of travellers' tales, reports back from real men who have ventured into the sorts of spaces their colleagues describe, accounts of how the realities of sexual politics have left a mark on their own lives. It should also, however, be read as a collective response to Shere Hite's call for a new kind of community of men, a discursive community in which men might cooperate in the analysis and rediscovery of their own gendered voices, and participate in the transformation of ideological constructs through the very personal struggles of their daily lives.

The first selection, a joint production of the members of an established men's group in Cambridge, England, offers a concrete example of what this might mean. In lieu of reading a paper at the original colloquium, these seven men led the audience in small-group workshops designed to provide a hands-on feel for what the work of their group was all about. Their purpose here is much the same: after an introduction to the group's origins, purpose, and daily workings, they share their reflections on specific issues that their participation in the group has brought to the fore. Their thoughts on such issues as childhood, work, parenting, sexuality, the body, and lived relations to feminism shed light not only on several men's personal experiences of manhood, but also on the long-term process by which they succeeded in recognizing, articulating, and grappling with them.

Martin Humphries' contribution, an engaging mosaic of narrative, analysis, and poetry, probes the resistances and resiliencies of the straight man's world from the perspective of a politically active gay socialist man. He begins by describing his experiences working with the men's publishing collective Achilles Heel. His candid personal account of a period of growth and self-questioning within a different kind of experimental male community leads him to reflect on his complex relation both to the straight men with whom he worked, and to the feminist ideals which they espoused. He then turns to the considerably less welcoming reception gay men have received in the broader community, where he develops a damning indictment against the endemic experience of homophobia, and the suggestion that certain forms of oppression against women and gay men might helpfully be viewed in a similar light.

Jeff Hearn addresses the most immediately visible form of such oppression in the phenomenon of sexual violence. Presenting a strong case against isolating men's personal, political, and theoretical responses to the issue, he takes up each perspective in turn to demonstrate the strengths and limitations of each approach in addressing it, as well as their ultimate interconnectedness. In a frank personal testimony, he presents his developing awareness of the constructedness of his own heterosexuality as one essential source of insight, and then turns to the history of men's political movements with and in response to feminism as focal points of collectivity and public action. Finally, he provides a useful overview of men's theoretical engagement with the problem of violence over the last twenty years as a means of appraising the contribution of gender theory to men's ongoing confrontation with the problem of their own sexuality.

None of the contributors to this volume offer simple remedies, and there is scarcely a point of doctrine on which all would agree. If there is a single consensus that runs through all nine of these pieces, it insists that such explorations must continue, that men, while remaining attentive to the changing directions and concerns of feminism, continue also to develop the alternative masculine voices that will enable them to speak – probing, recounting, questioning – the spaces in between, and to glimpse, perhaps, as well some of the ways that lie ahead.

NOTES

1 Upon receiving my invitation to participate in the colloquium, Germaine Greer commented to a mutual friend that, among other things, I might as well have arranged a series on 'Men and Menstrual Pains.' I'm still uncertain whether it was the conjunction that disturbed her or the terms that it connected, but she got me thinking about the title, for which I am grateful.

2 The same debt is apparent throughout Alice Jardine and Paul Smith's *Men in Feminism* (New York: Methuen, 1987), a book whose provocative title and contents have led to much fruitful discussion on the precise nature of this relationship. Joseph Boone's essay in the present volume offers reflections on this problem framed partly as a response to *Men in Feminism*.

3 These two essays (Bredbeck, Humphries), and several more dealing with other aspects of homosociality (Bristow, Hearn, Cambridge Men's Group) will evoke, perhaps, another sense of the 'between' in my title: that elaborated by Eve Kosofsky Sedgwick in her ground-breaking book *Between Men: English Literature and Male Homosocial Desire* (New York: Columbia University Press, 1985). It will be clear, in any case, that much of the writing in this volume is deeply indebted to her work.

Part I

Making space

Chapter 1

Of me(n) and feminism
Who(se) is the sex that writes?

Joseph A. Boone

Since the essay that follows was originally written in 1987 for inclusion in another essay collection, *Gender and Theory: Dialogues on Feminist Criticism* (1989), its reprinting here may benefit from a few words of explanation. First, despite the fact that it may initially read like a review-essay of Alice Jardine and Paul Smith's 1987 anthology, *Men in Feminism*, it was conceived in response to a much broader series of impressions I had been gathering for some time prior to the publication of the Jardine and Smith volume. *Men in Feminism* is best seen, then, as the *triggering* event, rather than sole offender or culprit, motivating me to articulate my uneasiness about the way in which men's relation to feminist criticism was at the time being politicized in academic circles. Since it seemed to me that a critical discourse had formed around the subject that almost necessarily precluded its potential, I decided to use the occasion of my essay to examine some of the stages whereby 'men and feminism' had become the 'issue,' the 'topic,' of the moment.

Even though the debate over men's relation to feminism has far from abated, I am relieved to discover that some of my most immediate worries seem less relevant in light of the several years that have intervened between the writing of this essay and its reappearance here. For in these five years an increasing number of male critics dedicated to the exploration of their gendered subject positions have begun *to do the work on*, not just theorize about, what I was then calling 'male feminist criticism,' and in the process they have begun to assemble an impressive array of methodologies for critiquing patriarchy, masculine subjectivity, and issues of sexuality in general. In face of this productivity, the issue of naming – whether to take on the label, for instance, of 'male feminism' – now strikes me as perhaps less urgent than measuring the degree of commitment to a feminist politics demonstrated in these men's newly engendered methods of analysis.

The lead essay in the collection *Men in Feminism* opens with an eye-catching assertion, one that is as provocative as it is literally and figuratively arresting. 'Men's relation to feminism,' Stephen Heath writes, 'is an impossible one. This is not said sadly nor angrily . . . but politically.'[1] Heath's claim to dispassionate objectivity and political correctness notwithstanding, the contents of this volume fairly bristle with the antagonistic emotions conjured forth by the subject matter announced in the controversial title of the volume – an antagonism fueled by the very wording of that title, in which the loaded preposition *in* is made to bear the weight of a rather questionable relation between men and feminism. But that relation, according to Heath, is also supposedly 'an impossible one,' and it is telling to note how Heath's formulation has set the tone for, as well as defined the limits of and boundaries to, nearly all the discussion that follows: one critic after the other in *Men in Feminism*, whatever his or her personal reading of the issue, nonetheless accedes to the *theoretical impossibility* of men ever being 'in' feminism except as an act of penetration, violence, coercion, or appropriation.

I'd like to suggest, however, that 'being *in*' isn't the only relation possible between men/feminism and redirect our attention to the *possibilities* (rather than impossibilities) inherent in the potential conjunction of men *and* feminism. For if we can find our way out of Heath's incapacitating metaphor of arrest, we may also find a way out of an equally incapacitating anger over the issue of inclusion/exclusion. This is not to ignore the very real political ramifications of questions of 'possibility' in a phallocentric world where power is still overwhelmingly male-identified; rather it is an attempt to chart a path whereby these points of contention, these potential limits, do not automatically bar our *thinking through* the issue of men and feminism. At the same time, I'd also like to suggest that theorizing the topic, as Heath and company often eloquently do, while it is obviously essential, also risks becoming essentializing; the issues suffusing the topic of men and feminism should not come to be perceived merely as a set of grammatical relations ('in' or 'for' or 'against'), at the expense of the simultaneously lived and practiced dimensions of that relation.

Thus, I'd like to risk personalizing the issue in the pages that follow, rather than leaving it an exclusively theoretical one. And one way of doing this, as the first half of my title suggests, will be to coax forth a bit of the 'me,' the personal pronoun hidden in the word *men*, the biologically determined category to which that pronoun also belongs – that individual 'me' in this case being the voice of a male literary critic who for years now has found in feminism a theory, praxis, and way of life that have become synonymous with his, my, sense of identity. In exposing the latent multiplicity and difference in the word *me(n)*, we can perhaps open up a space within the discourse of feminism where a male voice professing a feminist politics *can* have something to say beyond impossibilities and apologies and unresolved ire. Indeed, if the male critic can discover a position *from which* to speak that neither elides the importance of feminism to his work nor ignores the specificity of his gender, he may also find that his voice no longer exists as an abstraction, but that it in fact inhabits a body: its own sexual/textual body. In this regard, the really crucial question for feminists – male and female alike – is how to formulate terms for presenting the issue of 'men and feminism' so as not to limit its possibilities, overdetermine its body, from the outset.

And my analysis will begin with precisely this danger. For in the field of literary criticism in particular, it strikes me that to date the most important *public* discussions of the topic have been cast, however unconsciously, in terms of a two-dimensional opposition that has negatively structured our very perception of the issue, both as a theory and as a reality. In focusing on the disjunctions and alliances between men and the feminist movement in a specifically institutional sphere – that of academic criticism – I do not mean to give short shrift to those many other 'non-academic' contexts where feminism counters male opposition as well as encounters male support: instead I wish to suggest that those 'intellectual' debates that the public often conceives as (in both senses of the word) purely 'academic' are not without a certain charge for even the so-called real world: the rhetorical formations that underwrite rarified 'academic' theory may also illuminate the politics, and communicative impasses, that have accompanied the ongoing feminist struggle in its movement into the streets, the home, and the workplace.

In order to examine the debate surrounding men and feminism in my own 'workplace,' along with the premises underlying the articulation of that debate, I have chosen to focus on five seemingly random moments: (1) Elaine Showalter's publication of 'Critical Cross-Dressing' in 1983, the first prominent survey of the 'male feminist' phenomenon in literary criticism; (2) the panel 'Men in Feminism I & II' presented at the 1984 Modern Language Association Convention, the annual meeting to which tens of thousands of literature professors, willingly or not, flock; (3) another MLA panel on 'male feminist voices' in which I participated in 1986; (4) Alice Jardine and Paul Smith's editing of the *Men in Feminism* essay collection (stemming from the panel of the same name); and, finally, (5) Linda Kauffman's invitation that I participate in the essay collection, *Gender and Theory*, for which this essay was conceived. There is nothing absolute or binding about these stages, I hasten to emphasize, for they consist of events to which I have had very personal and indeed subjective relations – be it as friend, outsider, spectator, or contributor. But that is part of my point, for it has been in the very intimacies and awkwardnesses of my position in relation to each of these events that I have recurrently experienced the aforesaid gap between the 'me' and 'men' in 'me(n).' And, as the following section will now detail, it has been my experience of this discontinuity that has in turn inspired me to question the discursive formations in the literary critical institution whereby the concept of men and feminism, transformed into a territorial battlefield, has attained an 'impossible' status.

IMPOSSIBLE NARRATIVES

Although feminism has always remained acutely aware of its relation to men, the reverse situation hasn't necessarily been true. One of the insights of Elaine Showalter's witty 'Critical Cross-Dressing: Male Feminists and the Woman of the Year' was to pinpoint the formation of one such moment of reversal. For, by tapping into two seemingly unrelated cultural events to show the same masculine anxiety operating in both, Showalter proposed a link between an unexpected, and unexpectedly popular, phenomenon in several early 1980s films – the rise of the female impersonator or male heroine – and an equally unexpected phenomenon in academic circles – the avowal, by several prominent male literary critics, of their 'conversion' to feminist literary theory.[2] In particular, the pseudofeminism embodied in the film *Tootsie* (where Dorothy Michaels' *female* 'power,' after all is said and done, is only a *man's* masquerade) provided Showalter with a fascinating analogue for analyzing as instances of 'critical cross-dressing' the recently donned garb of feminist theory apparent in Jonathan Culler's *On Deconstruction* (1982) and Terry Eagleton's *The Rape of Clarissa* (1982). The irony of Culler's attempt to bring feminism positively to bear on deconstruction, Showalter points out, lies in his reluctance to foreground the relation of his own gender to such an endeavor; much as he advocates deconstruction's incorporation of feminist methods as a positive gain, he himself remains the untainted deconstructor, the removed and authorizing interpreter or 'analyst of feminist critical work' (126) who has (safely) positioned himself outside the feminist readings that he is, in actuality, often producing.[3] Showalter also points out how Eagleton's claim to find an ally for Marxist theory in feminism disguises a desire to compete with, dominate over, and ultimately arrogate feminism for his own agenda. Rather than a 'revolutionary' coupling of the two -*isms*, Eagleton's reading of *Clarissa* might be said to recapitulate a traditionally figured marriage, with the Marxist 'groom' ultimately silencing his feminist 'bride' by speaking over-loudly for and on behalf of her.

Through such perceptive readings, Showalter's review gives expression to the very understandable fear of the appropriation or 'raid' (129) of feminist criticism by male critics eager to cash in on its early successes. But Showalter's focus, from its very beginning, also unconsciously problematizes the issue she is investigating, by making what she calls the 'first wave of male feminist criticism' (131) appear synonymous with what is in fact a highly select group of critics – well-known and very powerful men in the academy already identified with specific schools of criticism other than feminist criticism and with strong pre-existing allegiances that have perhaps almost inevitably modified their professions of feminist sympathy. By not raising the possibility that the most empathetic, least appropriative male feminist practice might be happening *elsewhere* – away from public view, by precisely those men who lack the academic power, rank, or

numerous publications of Showalter's named 'cross-dressers' –
'Critical Cross-Dressing' therefore creates the illusion of a discursive field in which 'male feminism' can be perceived only in
terms of a struggle for power among superpowers (Showalter
versus Eagleton, say) and hence as potentially antagonistic,
intrusive, or threatening to those who have fought for years to
legitimize feminism within the academy. There is a catch here, of
course, for the problem is *not* Showalter's ignorance of an 'other
side' to male feminism, as many of her male colleagues and male
students can attest. The catch is in the simple fact that 'Critical
Cross-Dressing' was designated, from its beginnings, as a review
article of a handful of books published in 1982–83; and the trends
that Showalter finds in that published work, augmented by her
perception of the suspect 'feminism' of films like *Tootsie*, are
indeed congruent with her conclusions. The irony is that the
terms that her overview evolved out of its highly specific context
– that of the book review – quickly became for many other
feminists the basis for viewing the whole phenomenon of men
and feminism solely as one of appropriation: that is, of 'men *in*
feminism.'

In speaking of the contexts that shape a text's reception, however, I owe an explanation of the personal as well as institutional
contexts shaping my own reception of this article. In this case, the
'institutional' context was provided by Harvard's Center for
Literary Studies, which in the autumn of 1984 created its Feminist
Literary Theory Seminar – a 'first' in the university's tradition-
bound history. And the topic of discussion for the inaugural
meeting, as one of my colleagues, Marjorie Garber, informed me,
was to be Showalter's article. My initial excitement was brought
to a halt, however, when Marge apologetically added that,
against her own recommendation, men were specifically not
invited; some of the founding members felt that the topic was too
sensitive, that the women in the seminar needed to reach a group
consensus before opening its doors to men. 'But I'll pirate you my
copy of the essay,' Marge said with a complicitous wink. 'Under
the circumstances, I'd love to hear your reactions!' On the one
hand, I can't say that I didn't find it somewhat ironic that women
from as far away as Dartmouth and Wesleyan could come to my
institution to discuss 'male feminism,' while I – one of the only
nominally practicing 'male feminists' I knew on campus at the
time – could not. But, on the other hand, I'd been in the field too

long to dismiss lightly the claims of separatism at specific historical junctures, and so I tried to convince myself not to make too much out of this one incident. *Nonetheless*, as might well be imagined, the immediate result was that I read the Showalter article with special care, determined to discover my difference from the negatively represented 'male feminists' of the article's title. It's little wonder that 'Critical Cross-Dressing' came to mark a significant plateau in my perception of 'male feminism' as a more problematic issue than I'd previously experienced it to be.

These reflections are intimately connected to the second event that I have chosen to examine as a significant moment in the politicization of the concept of male feminism: the volatile double panel, organized under the title 'Men in Feminism: Men and Feminist Theory,' that took place at the 1984 MLA Convention in Washington, D.C. For, once again, it was a personal exchange – again involving my tenuous relation to Harvard and Harvard's tenuous relation to women's studies – that first brought this particular event to my attention. The setting for this exchange was a dinner held for one of the English Department's candidates for a women's studies position – exactly one week, incidentally, after the second meeting of the Feminist Literary Theory Seminar, to which men *had* been invited. Seated at a long table at a Cambridge restaurant named *Autre Chose*, Alice Jardine and I literally found ourselves *les autres*, shunted to the far end of the table so that the senior faculty members in attendance could grill the candidate from its center, as it were. It turned out to be a fortuitous exclusion from the dominant discourse, however, since it brought Alice and I into dialogue for the first time since we'd arrived on campus as beginning junior faculty. As we got to know each other, Alice mentioned the problems she was having coming up with a satisfactory response paper for an MLA panel she was on, a panel on men and feminism: she didn't find the two papers (Heath's and Smith's) she'd received very helpful, didn't want to come off sounding dictatorial or better-than-thou about what they, or other men interested in feminism, should be saying, but didn't want to let these guys entirely off the hook for being so persistently abstract either. Even now I can remember wondering why *these* men were the ones speaking to the subject if their views were so problematic, but at the time I decided to wait till the convention and judge for myself.

For, despite Alice's ambivalence (with which I could

empathize, given her position as respondent), the intention of the panel from my position (as one of its subjects) seemed entirely credible and potentially admirable – namely, to give voice to the growing perception among men and women alike that the increased participation of men in feminist discourse added a new if problematic dimension to the history of feminist criticism. But the very constitution of the panel, as I was to discover two weeks later, posed the enunciation of the problem in an equally problematic way. Male panelists – not Showalter's now (in)famous 'cross-dressers' but, as Jardine stressed, 'those men who are *really trying* . . . our allies' (56) – were invited by the panel's organizer, Paul Smith, to *theorize* about their relation to feminism for the first session, whereupon, in the second meeting, the female respondents took the men to task for theorizing rather than practicing what they preached. The collective response that emerged included a tone of general weariness at having, once again, to be the ones to say, in Alice's paraphrase, 'That's not quite it . . . you're not there yet' (54) and a shared suspicion that to the extent that men were 'there' in feminism at all, it was, again in Alice's words, 'to speak about "something else," some "larger issue"' (55).[4]

But while much of the criticism of male appropriations of feminist theory for 'larger' ends, as in Showalter's essay, was clearly on target, the very format of the two panels disturbingly seemed to reproduce the two-sided opposition against which the feminist concept of difference ideally sets itself: men as a unified body visually and temporally set against women as a unified body; men speculating about 'entering' the ranks of feminist women; and the latter reprimanding the former for their bad behavior, 'rather tired' (88) imitations of feminist theory, and 'all too familiar' (72) arguments 'which do not take us very far' (71). In effect, potential dialogue had become confrontation between two 'sides' aligned by gender, sides whose interaction was thereby doomed to reinforce stereotypes of both sexes (men blunder in, women scold). In the process the question of differences within and between the men's perspectives, to say nothing of the differences in the women's points of view, were set aside.

Sitting in the audience, eager to see an issue so close to home being treated seriously yet frustrated by its very airing, I experienced a series of contradictory reactions. First of all, throughout the men's talks, I kept thinking how they were *not* speaking for me, for the 'me' in 'men,' or, for that matter, for my male friends; in particular, Heath's and Smith's attempts to intellectualize their relation to feminism seemed a detour for setting that relation into practice – for all their words and wordplays, for all their confessional techniques, their texts seemed void of any body, any immediate presence. During the question period that followed and intermittently throughout the second panel, moreover, I found myself siding with the women's anger against those hypothesized male entrepreneurs jumping on the 'feminist theory bandwagon' (57) now that most of the groundwork had been done; the intrusiveness of such critics happened at my expense too, I found myself thinking; I had 'been there' years before the arrival of these belated converts, with their too-easy criticism and how-to mandates. And yet a third impression simultaneously set in, for, as the female critiques accelerated, I began to feel a belated sympathy for the actual men (rather than the hypothesized appropriators) who had participated in the morning's session. They, after all, by virtue of their age and lack of professional status alone, were far from being the 'born-again' Bandwagoners or 'Divide and Conquerors' (56) under censure, and yet the format they had either helped organize or agreed to participate in was setting them up, it struck me, in a no-win situation.[5] As I left the panel, I kept trying to imagine where my voice fit in the spectrum I had just witnessed, and, more pointedly, which of the two panels I would have chosen to participate in, had I had the choice: in either case, in my case, in the case of feminist scholarship at large, *whose* is the sex, finally, that speaks?

I had my chance to appear on the other side of the podium two years later, when I was asked by Laura Claridge and Elizabeth Langland to moderate an MLA panel they were arranging on 'Male Feminist Voices within a Patriarchal Language' – the focus this time around being on the 'sympathetic' male writer, rather than the male critic, attempting to write in a non-phallic mode. At the time I couldn't imagine a more ideal situation. Laura and Elizabeth were seeking a moderator in name so that they could at once organize the panel and present papers on it, and thus I would get a free trip to the MLA with a minimal amount of work – merely introducing the session and the speakers. Moreover, the panel's prospectus struck me as very much a step in the right direction. It suggested that we locate the male voice as a third or odd term in a gendered discourse that consists of (at least) man, woman, and the dominant cultural ideology that we call patriarchy: that is, maleness needn't be assumed to be coeval with patriarchy, with woman symmetrically positioned on the other side of the proposition. But the very construction of the panel – as I found when I read the selected papers – tended to blur this important move and reinstate, once again, a male–female opposition. Part of the problem was, simply, the plain old element of chance that enters into the arrangement of any panel. For it so happened, first, that all the chosen panelists were women (although both men and women applied) and, second, that all their papers, while excellent, nonetheless focused on *men writing about women*. Whether the subject was Shelley on feminine ideality, Emerson on Margaret Fuller, Forster on the Schlegel sisters, or Hardy on Tess, 'male sympathy' was shown to transform itself into a form of linguistic appropriation as the authorial voice inevitably became entangled with the patriarchal rhetoric against which it was ostensibly rebelling.[6]

Such critiques, however applicable to these authors, couldn't begin to address a number of other questions that such a panel might have opened up. What difference, for instance, might the perspective of a man on the panel have made? Had any panelists – male or female – examined a male author's exploration of his own sexuality, might a more 'authentic' male – as opposed to phallocentric and appropriative – desire have been located? What of the male writer writing from a gay or otherwise marginalized perspective of race or class? (Forster, the one homosexual author under consideration, was examined, tellingly, only in regard to his views on women, not on how his difference from a heterosexual male norm might have influenced that relation.) And even when the male writer focuses on the 'feminine,' might there be alternatives beyond 'appropriation' – instances, however rare, when he has let femaleness transform, redefine, his textual erotics, allowed himself *to be read through* femininity and femaleness, rather than seeking to become the authorizer speaking on its behalf?

Having unconsciously precluded an exploration of these differences – the modalities of position that would have indeed rendered man as a third or odd term for analysis in the investigation of gendered discourses – the panel's very constitution had in fact reconstituted 'man' as a homogeneous entity, the 'fall-guy' for a one-sided rather than really radical deconstruction. Moreover, as the one man on stage, I found the question of position all the more immediate. There I was, by virtue of having been listed in the program as the panel's moderator and having introduced its speakers, in the perceived position of having selected this panel, endorsed its version of 'male feminism,' and authorized four women to speak to the subject (a double-bind: not only for potentially offending some women by seeming to assume a 'male' right to authorize their voices, but equally for offending some men by seeming to cede their story, their voices, to women). And yet there I was, just the same, the one male among four women on stage and the one person whose participation was peripheral to the main event in a discussion, ironically enough, of male feminist voices.

Beyond panels often lie essay collections-in-the-making, which has proved to be the case for both the panels I've mentioned: we now have Jardine and Smith's *Men in Feminism*, and Claridge and Langland's *Out of Bounds: Male Writing and Gender(ed) Criticism* has recently appeared as well.[7] The fourth stage I would like to examine in the emerging academic discourse on men and feminism centers on the way in which a widely read anthology like *Men in Feminism* can unconsciously limit what might be said about men's participation in feminist criticism. For I would suggest that as a totality *Men in Feminism* almost unwittingly seems to recapitulate the problems inherent in the panel from which it originated. Telling in this regard is the semi-apologetic tone of the brief introduction written by the co-editors, Jardine and Smith. For while they seem to agree in feeling the 'question of "men in feminism" [to be] a relatively unpromising one' (vii), they do not *restate* the issue to make it less 'unpromising' or less problematic, either for themselves or for their potential readership. Another warning sign emerges a few lines later, when they announce that 'it became clear almost immediately . . . that most (though, finally, not all) of our contributors would be straight, white academics,' which they admit to be one of the book's limitations (viii). Just why or how the latter fact 'became clear almost immediately' gave me pause when I first read it: who, I wondered, had they sought out as potential contributors? For what seems 'unpromising' or limited here is not so much the topic itself as any *framing* of the question (symbolized in the deliberate retention of the controversial title, 'men *in* feminism') that would make it 'clear almost immediately' that most of its male contributors would more likely than not be men 'in(to)' feminism in the most troublesome sense of the word.[8]

As if in confirmation of this suspicion, the collection includes as 'experts' on the subject Jacques Derrida, Robert Scholes, Denis Donoghue (in small print), and Terry Eagleton (in reply to Showalter) – prominent critics whose relation to feminism has never gone unquestioned. In opting for name-recognition by including such men among the seven added male contributors, the editors merely reproduced the problem that I've already noted in relation to Showalter's essay: for the price of spotlighting 'famous' names as *the* representatives of a movement that inevitably forms elsewhere than in the dominant discourse is to risk precluding what can be said differently, other than in the language of the 'straight, white academic.' Given this set-up, there's a certain uncanny poetic justice to the fact that, by the last essay in the collection, Jardine's 'bandwagon' has been transformed by Rosi Braidotti into a veritable 'bulldozer': 'Blinded by what *they* have learned to recognize as "theory," *they* bulldoze their way through feminism . . . *They* are walking all over us . . . "*They*" are the best male friends we [women]'ve got, and "*they*" are not really what we had hoped for' (234–35; emphasis added). Braidotti's very rhetoric of repetition has transformed 'men' into an army of indistinguishable, unnamed 'they's'; in the process any idea of 'me(n)' has vanished altogether.

The problem of choosing one's contributors – an editorial problem not unrelated, of course, to the exigencies of the marketplace – takes on a different slant when one turns to the female critics not originally on the panel but included in *Men in Feminism* and to the way that, as a group, their essays construct – or avoid – the subject of 'male feminism' itself.[9] For example, Naomi Schor's 'Dreaming Dissymmetry: Barthes, Foucault, and Sexual Difference' strikes me as superb criticism, one of the best essays in the entire collection; nonetheless, by virtue of its rather exclusive focus on Barthes and Foucault, it has the effect of shifting the discussion from 'male feminism' to yet more examples of – if we stretch our imagination – men 'into' feminism. Instead of Showalter's Anglo-American cross-dressers, we get, this time round, an elite class of male French poststructuralists whose fascination with castrati and hermaphrodites becomes the basis for theories of sexual discourse that ultimately enforce dreams of sexual 'in-difference' (in Schor's apt phrase), of a lost paradise of blissful indeterminacy that transcends sexual specificity. But in so attempting to move *beyond* difference, Barthes and Foucault in effect also *refuse* feminism's claim of female difference, leading Schor to generalize that 'no feminist theoretician *who is not also a woman* has ever fully espoused the claims to a feminine specificity ... Even the most enlightened among the male feminists condone claims to female specificity only as a temporary tactical necessity' (109; emphases added). While Schor's reading of Barthes's and Foucault's displacement of sexual difference is right on target, this larger generalization, however, depends on what is in fact a highly selective focus of two. Indeed, the trajectory of Schor's argument unconsciously repeats the *clinamen*, or 'shift away from' (103), of which she accuses Barthes and Foucault – a swerve in argument whereby two men with only an implicit relation to feminism are transformed into universal exemplars of 'even the most enlightened . . . male feminists,' *all* of whom, it would appear, have gotten it wrong.

Another of the collection's highlights is Nancy Miller's unpacking of the male anger hidden behind platitudes of universal judgment in Denis Donoghue's attacks on Gilbert and Gubar's *Norton Anthology of Literature by Women* in the *New Republic*.[10] But, like Schor's essay, Miller's 'Man on Feminism' in the long run gives us only what her title announces: *a* man, *one* man unfortunately speaking for too many men, holding forth *on* feminism, certainly *not* speaking on behalf of the male feminist. By definition, then, Miller's essay addresses not the subject or practice of male feminism, but rather its antithesis. Nonetheless, I would suggest, the specific terms of the case she makes against Donoghue *do* turn out to be highly relevant to the hidden imperatives shaping this collection's presentation of that subject. For in revealing the way in which Donoghue's gripe with feminism actually disguises his battle with poststructuralist theory 'over ownership of (literary) discourse' (141) – that is, a struggle between the Big Daddies of Humanism and Deconstruction, in which feminist criticism serves as the pretext, the agency of mediation – Miller's argument made me realize the degree to which many of the contributors to *Men in Feminism* use the subject 'male feminism' in much the same way, as *their* pretext to wage other critical wars. In the process, ironically, 'male feminism' comes to occupy in structural terms the traditional position of women in patriarchy – the ultimately expendable item of exchange that merely gets the conversation going. No wonder my vague discomfort, then, with several of these selections. For it is not that any of them is 'bad,' but that they often have other, hidden, or not-so-hidden, agendas. Thus, for example, when Jane Gallop uses the occasion of her essay to unmask the sexism of Jean Baudrillard's theories of seduction, it turns out that her real interest is in addressing the relation of French theory to feminism (the idea of men and feminism, or even anti-feminism, has entirely dropped out of the picture by the last paragraph). Likewise, Robert Scholes's 'Reading Like a Man' actually serves more as an occasion to attack Culler's deconstructive practice (in reading 'as a woman') than as any kind of exploration of the subject announced in his title (broached only in his concluding sentence). In the end, it is no surprise that *Men in Feminism* becomes a territorial battlefield, reproducing the discursive thrusts of its title, when the very issues at stake have been so clouded, disguised, or otherwise silenced.

My criticisms notwithstanding, it is also important to note the collection's many merits, not the least being the very fact of its having raised the issue in the first place – and 'first' statements are always more difficult to make. Not only does it include Schor and Miller's excellent work and Alice Jardine's sorely needed outline of what a male feminist praxis might really include, but it features the thoughtful commentary of three added male critics – Richard Ohmann, Cary Nelson, and Craig Owens. Indeed, with more contributions like these, the volume would have avoided the pitfalls that I have sketched above.[11] The Claridge and Langland volume also moves beyond its panel format in promising directions; several male contributors, none easily assimilable to the other, are included, some of whom write about male writers' encoding of male experience.

But the danger is always there of reinstating those potentially blinding symmetries that a feminist understanding of difference should instead encourage us all as feminists to unravel, to move beyond. Thus, as a kind of coda to this part of my essay, I'd like to present a vignette that has to do with the form – and formulation – of Linda Kauffman's 1989 *Gender and Theory: Dialogues on Feminist Criticism*, the collection for which this essay was conceived. One of Linda's agendas, as I understood it, was to give voice to less well-known critics; another was to redress the imbalances of the *Men in Feminism* collection, and the format of essay-plus-response was self-consciously conceived as a means of making an ongoing *dialogue* part of that redressing process. Yet, curiously, what did I find when I looked back at the wording of the letter I received inviting me to become a contributor? Inevitably: 'the collection is arranged so that *male essayists* are responded to by *feminist theorists*, and vice versa, and presently includes the following . . . ' (emphases added). 'Male essayists' versus 'feminist theorists'; once again, two sides of a divide, leaving me unclear where *I*, claiming to be both 'male' and 'feminist,' belong. For note, the wording does not stipulate '*female* feminist theorists,' although that is the obvious, albeit perhaps unintentional, implication, since all of 'the following' in Linda's letter turn out to be male–female pairs. So I have chosen, for my peace of mind, to take advantage of this slight opening in phraseology and, rather than considering myself one of the 'male essayists,' to include myself among the 'feminist theorists' – not that I prefer being considered more of a 'theorist' than an 'essayist,' but in hopes of creating a bit of healthy confusion, a field of imaginative play that might contribute to the liberation of our current discourses on and around the subject of 'men and feminism.' For, when it comes to feminist criticism, I repeat, only half facetiously, whose *is* the sex that writes?

POSSIBLE NARRATIVES

I'd now like to pick up on various hints strewn throughout the prior commentary that, if stitched together, might help shift the direction that the issue of men and feminism has hitherto followed and, in the process, redirect our attention to various areas from which a critical practice by men invested in a feminist politics might logically *emerge* rather than sink in (Heathian) impossibility. The following, of course, is only a partial list.

1   One such directive is for concerned literary feminists to stop looking to prominent figures like Derrida for the final word on men's potential to theorize their relation to feminist theory and practice. This is not to say that Derrida's wish to 'write as a Woman' or Culler's prescriptions for 'reading as a woman reading as a woman' might not be of interest; but it is to

suggest that more relevant scholarly work – work more aptly described as feminist and worthy of feminists' attention – is being carried on elsewhere.

2 Second, we need to account for an important generational factor if we are to begin to measure with more discrimination the multiplicities of men's relations to feminism. For, as Andrew Ross has rightly pointed out, there are now 'men [in academics] young enough for feminism to have been a primary component of their intellectual formation.'[12] The emergence of a whole generation of young men educated in feminism does not in itself allay the problem of confiscation or appropriation, but it does, I would argue, create a scenario qualitatively different from the 'Bandwagoning' or 'Divide and Conquer' theories of male feminism offered by Jardine and others. Such theories generally are more applicable to male critics with, as Ross puts it, a significant 'pre-feminist' past, who thus tend to respond to feminism as either an alluring 'other' or an overwhelming threat, or both at once. Moreover, if the presence of feminist-educated men makes a difference, so too, potentially, does its correlative: that there are now young women in the academy whose education in feminism has at least partially been shaped by men with feminist interests, both in their lives and their scholarship. Again, this is not to say that this new situation does not pose its own dangers, but simply to recognize a reality, one that has already begun to shift the way in which our current students – tomorrow's scholars – will think of men's participation in feminist studies.

3 A third, related point that has emerged from what I've had to say thus far concerns the danger of lumping all 'men' together as a uniform category. What I hope we've begun to learn in this regard is that all feminists, male and female alike, need to be particularly attentive to those marginalized male voices whose interests may intersect with, or move along paths that are congruent to, but not the same as, those already marked out by feminist interests to date. If men are to take to heart Jardine's warning against the 'suppression of the diversity and dis-agreement within the [feminist] movement itself' (57), women and men alike need to keep the same principle in mind when judging the possibilities of a male feminist critical activity, its own potential for diversities, divergence, and disagreement.

This recognition is exactly what Stephen Heath elides when he resigns himself to the belief that men's attempts at a 'male writing' can only reproduce itself, turn out more of the 'same.' Tellingly, he leaves unexplored a parenthetical qualification that he inserts at this very moment: '(unless perhaps [such writing emerges] in and from areas of gay men's experience . . .)' (25).

For, at this historical juncture, many of the men in the academy who are feminism's most supportive 'allies' *are* gay. Somehow this fact and its implications have often been forgotten in many of the discussions surrounding the 'male feminist' controversy, especially those represented in the *Men in Feminism* volume. From Heath's to Braidotti's essays, too many of the generalizations made about men's desire to become a part of feminism *take for granted* the 'heterosexual' basis of that desire – the predominant imagery of penetration is but one clue to the preponderance of these assumptions. In contrast, a recognition of the presence and influence of gay men working in and around feminism has the potential of rewriting feminist fears about 'men *in* feminism' as a strictly heterosexual gesture of appropriation. The annual conference of the five-year-old Center for Lesbian and Gay Studies at Yale, while not without its own discursive struggles, has gone far to dispel such fears. Indeed, what impressed me most about the center's inaugural conference, held in 1987, was the extent to which 'gay studies' as an intellectual event was able to begin at a highly sophisticated, theoretical level precisely because of the informing influence of feminism; what I saw demonstrated throughout was a convergence of feminist method and gay studies – epitomized in the conference's presiding intellectual 'presence,' Eve Sedgwick – in the service of creating a discipline and an agenda that claim to be neither superior to nor the same as feminism, but rather in an ever-present relation of contiguity with the originating politics of feminism.

Hence, in acknowledging the possible plurality of male feminist voices, gay or otherwise defined, along with the many possible directions that such work might take, we would do well to recall Nancy Miller's caution to those who would reduce the feminist enterprise to a pat formula, bearing in mind the potential applicability of her words to male feminist criticism as well: 'feminist criticism is not about more of the same. It is about the imagination of difference that does not break down into two agendas, but [that] opens onto a complicated map of contiguities' (141–42).

As with any political theory, there is always, of course, the very real danger of feminism being used irresponsibly by men, particularly when it leaves its established domains. Thus, I'd like to close this essay with a few observations, garnered from my own subjective experiences, that other male academics interested in feminist criticism might consider.

1 My first impulse is simply to encourage men to *identify with* feminism, taking on without fuss or ado the label of 'feminist' if that's indeed your interest and appropriate to the work you're producing. Too many people, men and women, shy away from the appellation as if the word had the power to diminish their scholarship. A feminist politics, to the contrary, is about taking risks, about assuming the responsibility of a name or label, if only as a temporary political strategy.[13]

2 Second, men participating in feminism should make their own oppressive structures (ideological, social, psychological) *present* for critique, rather than hiding them under a veil of abstract musing. Part of this process, for example, is simply to remember the multiple ways in which the 'me' in 'me(n)' – whose cause I've been advocating all along – is nonetheless gendered male, *does* belong, after all, to the biological and social group 'men.' This is an identification for which, at some point, all of us feminist men must take responsibility. What, for example, happens when we academic 'me(n)' must take part in specifically male spheres of action or power? To what degree do we choose to disguise, or not, our commitments to feminism? How do we sometimes take advantage of our born status as 'men' to negotiate the treacherous process of establishing a professional identity and continuing to exist within the limitations of our specific institutional circumstances? Whenever such circumstances tempt us to 'pass' as 'men' rather than as 'me(n),' what do we do with, where do we leave, our female allies?

3 Third, men with a commitment to a feminist politics need to be willing to forge self-definitions of themselves as men that make room for the acknowledgment of a difference and a sexuality that is truly heterogeneous. Which means, really, to

quote Jardine quoting Hélène Cixous, *that men still have every-thing to say about their sexuality.* This is one of the logical, crucial, and, I hope, inevitable directions in which an en-lightened discourse of masculinity will develop. For instance, what do the texts we men read and produce and teach say – or avoid saying – about the relation of son to father, man to his gendered subjectivity, to his physical body, to his homoeroti-cism, to desire and its multiple effects on his and others' pleasures? In this regard, I find Jardine's entire list of 'appro-priate' areas of exploration for the would-be male feminist in her essay in *Men in Feminism* right to the point. My only caveat is that many of these have already been put into practice by the male critics I know, men who, in Jardine's phrase, are learning 'to speak as . . . body-coded male[s]' (60) precisely in order to re-imagine man. Which is inevitably to change the shape of patriarchy and its discourses as well.

4 Such acts, hence, are not only theoretical but also political, which ties in with a final observation I'd like, tentatively, to make. Women in the feminist movement have for two decades successfully shared their ideas collectively, seeking each other out in communal networks of relationship. How eventful it would be if more men professing a politics grounded in feminism did likewise. This is not to suggest we should begin forming exclusive men's clubs (that would indeed be only to produce more of the same), but to remind ourselves that we can learn from each other, as well as from our female friends. I would like to think that such a phenomenon – men really trusting men – would signal a cataclysmic change in the structures of our contemporary society, dealing the traditional notion of the Old Boys' Network a blow from which it might, I hope, never recover.

But my friend Patsy Yaeger, reading this essay, said musingly: here is the one point in your paper where I begin to feel un-comfortable and need to be convinced by something more; how can you trust groups of men not to repeat the old order, or not to erase women altogether in forming their cozy communities? I hesitate, too: I want to assure Patsy that the 'me(n)' for whom I've been speaking are different, not indifferent to such dangers. Then I think back to my hypothesis, following my reading of Nancy Miller's essay, of the way in which our current discourses on 'male feminism' have already constituted such men as the odd element, the expendable item of exchange, in current critical debates; and, to the degree that truly feminist-minded men also occupy the position of outsider in the homosocial transactions that make up patriarchy, perhaps, just perhaps, the linking together of their, our, individualities is to establish a counter-network of exchange necessarily subversive of traditional masculine networks of power. A community with phalluses, rather than the community as Phallus, need exist only as a threat to the existing patriarchal order, not to women individually or to feminism as a movement. So I tell myself, telling Patsy, but I don't know: this may be my dream of utopia (as opposed to Barthes' or Foucault's), marking in fact an 'impossible' limit beyond which male feminism cannot go – and yet, even so, that limit of possibility is one that I'd like, for now, for me, for men, to keep in view.

NOTES

This essay first appeared in a slightly longer version in *Gender and Theory: Dialogues on Feminist Criticism*, ed. Linda Kauffman (London and New York: Basil Blackwell, 1989); it was then reprinted, in the present version, in *Engendering Men: The Question of Male Feminist Criticism*, ed. Joseph A. Boone and Michael Cadden (New York and London: Routledge, 1990). I am grateful for the comments given and interest shown in this essay when presented, in various stages of its composition, at Princeton University, Dartmouth College, the Graduate Center of the City University of New York, and the Feminist Doctoral Colloquium of the English Department at Harvard.

1 Stephen Heath, 'Male Feminism,' in *Men in Feminism*, ed. Alice Jardine and Paul Smith (London and New York: Methuen, 1987), p. 1. All further references to the essays in this collection appear in the text in parentheses.

2 Elaine Showalter, 'Critical Cross-Dressing: Male Feminists and the Woman of the Year,' *Raritan* (Fall 1983), reprinted in *Men in Feminism*, pp. 116–32. Page references are to the latter.

3 Despite theoretical problems I have with Jonathan Culler's attempt to talk about 'reading as a woman' in *On Deconstruction*, my intuition is that he is a genuinely sympathetic ally of feminism, and I should not like my repetition of Showalter's criticisms to come to stand in my readers' minds for the person, a man who might be very different from the written traces embedded in a document composed nearly a decade ago. The same goes for all the critics I mention in the course of this essay, from Stephen Heath on: I am not judging, when I criticize, the individual person or critic, but rather his or her

historical *participation,* at a given moment in time (a panel, a paper, a publication), in the articulation of a discourse on men and feminism that may extend beyond that critic's intention or awareness.

4 Among the men, two of the panelists, Paul Smith and Stephen Heath, were generally perceived as positioning themselves as outsiders wishing to be 'in'/to feminism, while the third, Andrew Ross, avoided any direct commentary on his role as a male feminist by offering a specific case-analysis of sexual difference. In addition to Jardine, the women's panel included Judith Mayne, Elizabeth Weed, and Peggy Kamuf. All of their essays are reprinted in *Men in Feminism.* It should be added that Heath's essay, 'Male Feminism,' pp. 1–32, which circulated among all the panelists before the convention, is not the same as his final presentation paper ('Men in Feminism: Men and Feminist Theory,' pp. 41–46), which, significantly, omits the opening argument about the 'impossibility' of men entering feminism and, in critiquing Smith and Derrida, attempts to refute the whole inclusion/exclusion proposition. But the fact was that everyone's earlier reading of Heath's original essay ensured that its discursive positionings were palpably *present* throughout the double session, both in rhetorical terms (as others quoted or cited the opinions expressed in it) and on an emotional level.

5 Not only did the format work to the men's detriment, it also channeled the earned authority of these women to criticize the men's arguments into a depressingly traditional 'feminine' role: their authority suddenly capable of *appearing* merely that of the nagging mother scolding her wayward sons, their authority voicing itself only secondarily or reactively, in response to men's words – a point Jardine (54) and Weed (71) also make.

6 The papers were Laura Claridge's 'Shelley's Poetics: The Female as Enabling Silence,' Christina Zwarg's 'Emerson as "Mythologist" in *The Memoirs of Margaret Fuller Ossoli,*' Margaret Higgonet's 'Hardy's Tess – An Exchange of Voice,' and Elizabeth Langland's 'E. M. Forster's Right Rhetoric: The Omniscient Narrator as Female in *Howards End.*' The two panelists whom Claridge and Langland selected out of those who responded to the call for papers, Zwarg and Higgonet, wrote extremely subtle and probing essays well worth inclusion on the panel; the irony is not in the quality of any of these presentations *individually* but in the way that *collectively* they delimited the topic announced in the session's title.

7 Alice Jardine and Paul Smith's *Men in Feminism* was published in 1987 by Routledge, New York; *Out of Bounds* by Laura Claridge and Elizabeth Langland was published in 1990 by Massachusetts UP.

8 At this point in my original essay, I included an endnote in which I drew up a then hypothetical 'table of contents' of gender-oriented work by male literary critics that might have formed a more 'promising' volume. (That list became the starting point for the essay collection I eventually co-edited with Michael Cadden, *Engendering Men,* cited above.) In a response paired with my essay in Kauffman's volume, Toril Moi seizes upon this endnote to cinch her argument

that my essay 'is littered with comments antagonistic to older men or to men who are speaking when he is not.' That is, by relegating this list to 'a footnote which does nothing but list *twenty*(!) names of deserving "invisible" men,' I in effect silence their voices ('does nothing but') and ensure their continued 'invisibility' (187). I trust that *Engendering Men* – with its sixteen quite visible essays by men 'speaking when I am not' – goes some way in disproving Moi's conspiracy theory. (True confessions: for a long time I fantasized publishing a response to Moi's response titled – to pun on my own title – 'Of *Moi* and Feminism: The Terrifying Toril' – a response in which I would analyze the series of rather aggressive attacks that Moi has leveled against a number of American feminists, particularly those whose work disproves the American/Continental opposition she constructs in *Sexual/Textual Politics*. But I'll leave well enough alone by containing my fantasy within these parentheses, in an aside relegated, appropriately enough, to a – merely – 'silent' note.)

9 These included, in addition to a reprint of Showalter's *Raritan* essay, essays by Nancy Miller, Naomi Schor, Jane Gallop, Meaghan Morris, and Rosi Braidotti. I suspect that part of the problem I sense here has to do with the fact that some of these essays were either written or conceived before they were solicited for this collection – hence the degree to which they might not directly address the issue at hand.

10 Donoghue's review is reprinted in *Men in Feminism* after Miller's article 'for the reader's convenience' (138); whether or not to include the piece was much deliberated by the editors, who ultimately decided Miller's analysis couldn't be understood without its referent. The 'compromise' was to print the review in small type, in order to set it off from the other contributions.

11 I like the way in which Richard Ohmann's and Cary Nelson's titles ('In, With' and 'Men, Feminism: The Materiality of Discourse,' respectively) attempt to subvert what might be called the prepositional impasse of the collection's title; such plays with the pernicious *in* of 'men in feminism,' nonetheless, attest to the shaping influence the concept has exerted over the entire collection.

12 Ross makes this comment in a follow-up response to his original essay for the *Men in Feminism* volume (p. 86); all the original panelists were invited to contribute responses, one of its innovative features.

13 As I suggest in my opening comments, my perception of the issue of 'naming' or 'labeling' has evolved considerably since I first wrote this essay. In many ways the introduction that Michael Cadden and I wrote to *Engendering Men* begins at this point in order to move beyond it, suggesting that our enterprise is still in search of its '(im)proper name' and that its relationship to established feminist criticism thus necessarily – and perhaps fruitfully – remains 'in question.'

Chapter 2

Why can't a good man be sexy?
Why can't a sexy man be good?

Naomi Segal

The paper that follows arose out of both personal and theoretical preoccupations. Given as the first talk in a well-publicized series with a challenging overall theme, its title drew an audience of a size that shocked even the organizers. More than a hundred people – most of them fresh-faced undergraduates – crowded into a room half the required size, hoping perhaps to hear the problem solved or see a Gordian knot sliced before their eyes. The paper, like the title, however, consists almost entirely of questions. It is written overtly from the position of a feminist mother, and it offers no advice. It does not pretend to debate anything but subjective problems, but it assumes that subjectivities coexisting in an institution bring objectively real and generally relevant problems into existence. These are questions of rights and boundaries but also of desire. Desire is what we do not control; goodwill and desire are perhaps, peculiarly and sadly, twins that sit incompatibly in the domestic nest.

Re-editing the paper a year after I first delivered it, I approach it with a certain sense of the uncanny – last year's news both distant and too familiar. The question on which the paper ended – where is the space where the two men can be one man? – may be read as utopian or merely pessimistically rhetorical. I shall return, in some closing remarks, to my more recent thoughts on the subject. For now, I shall suggest that one cause for the split between the good and the sexy may simply be the natural invidiousness of habit: living with anyone or anything leads to the familiarity that breeds if not contempt, at least inattention. Sexual desire must be attentive. The kind of attention it requires is both other-directed and narcissistic – and daily contact may blur both of these in a way that conscious effort could remedy. Yet how is it that our children continue to be beautiful in a way wholly other than sexual and which develops through trials and errors but without fading away? What is it about adults living together that can blunt the mutual gaze of two equals with good intentions? Are we simply the slaves of the history of our institutions or our psychology? Knowing what is wrong can be the crucial first step to change – or it can be recognition that only dissolution may allow something new to begin. Either way, the next step must be knowing what we want, and hoping they and we might want in the same ways . . . .

The problem of feminism was and remains men. The problem I have in mind here is not that of men as oppressors but – the personal being as much political as ever – rather that of the men we love, and how we love them. (When I use the term 'love' I do it in the full awareness of how old-fashioned it sounds – this need not detain us – and how complicated it is; but it is love that is at issue here, along with the apparently more simple problem of desire.)

Homosexual love is, of course, no easier to work out in this respect – in fact within feminism the moral debates that rage most urgently at present are those among lesbians about their modes of desire, fantasy and behaviour – and perhaps homosexual love is both clearer and more irresoluble as an issue. But the issue of desire for heterosexual feminists, and how to live that desire in love (and whether these two are necessarily, as the Romantics told us, mutually contradictory), is compounded by the problems of living in a conventionally endorsed institution. Whether actually married or cohabiting as parents, men and women who try to live feminism together seem driven up against a set of massive problems. Let's take marriage as our paradigm, for in it the institution is fully in place. However little we might change our names, when feminist women enter into that partnership that is supposed (and that we expect) to provide support of several kinds and a continued kind of loving, how do we reckon to make it consistent with our ideology? Can marriage take in equality? What do we mean by equality? Are there some aspects of our wifehood that we want intact, along with our outdoor freedoms? Do we, in any case, get enough of these freedoms not to resent the token man we choose to live with? And as for children – how can we, as strange as this may sound, combine heterosexuality with maternity? Can we combine motherhood with parenthood? Who is the father of our children?

My title is not just a good hook for audience or reader. It is, I think, the crucial issue now for men and women who are feminists. How are desire and work to be combined in the home? Can they be? If not, why can't they be?

More questions. Who *are* the men we call good? Who are the men we call sexy? Where do they come from? What parenting (what mothering) made them as they are – or as they seem to us, because of course the good and the sexy may only be in the eyes of the beholder, it may be the case that one woman's good man is another woman's sexy man, and if this is so, perhaps parenting has a less inexorable effect than the institutions we live in in adulthood. By 'goodness' – another wonderfully old-fashioned term – I mean feminist goodness, what we sixties children call 'right-on-ness,' the political scruples we expect of men we choose to live with, something that may, common sense tells us, be more readily found in certain gay men than in heterosexual men – but *why*? Is there something wrong with heterosexual desire? Is there something wrong with the work-sharing institution we mean by marriage? Yes, of course, both. But what are we to do about it?

Is goodness incompatible with masculinity – and if it is, for whom? For us in our modes of desire? For men in their sense of self? Can a good father only ever feel he is an inadequate mother? We may laugh at his tussling with this, but if we do it is unkind and evasive laughter, evasive of something jealous in ourselves. Do we really want our children's father to take over those aspects of motherhood – sensuality and passion – that we most prize? (There are, of course, real dangers of a predatory incestuous interest if they do, something we feel easily innocent of, even though predatoriness and incest may both come in various forms.) If we don't want our men to get this close to our children, what kind of fatherhood are we leaving them? What kind of sensuality and passion are we leaving them?

What is the difference between being a wife (despised and painful term) and a mother? Is the husband of a feminist doomed to perceive himself between these two metaphorical poles? And there is more – for we all know how difficult it is to have a son. How are we to bring up our sons – how are their fathers to bring up our sons – in such a way that they can be both good and sexy?

The split in my title is shocking in part because, with a quick reverse of gender, we can see it as the mainstay of the patriarchal ideology: *maman* or *putain*, virgin (that is, desexualized mother) or whore, it is the crudest of political snares. For a feminist to propose a similar split, she has first to be clear that we are not, of course, in control of our desiring imaginations (this is the not-so-secret secret of any committed politics) and secondly to try and show that when this dichotomy is spoken from the point of view of the subordinated group it has quite new connotations. Or has it? Can we always rely on the virtue of the victim to get us by morally? Or are we oppressors in that place so long assigned to us and to which we, like all working people, inevitably return, the hearth and home? Or again, if we accuse ourselves, are we too succumbing to the temptation of seeing the mother as that force of nature that has too uncanny a power not to be, by very definition, destructive?[1] Why should the bad habit of mother-blaming stop, after all, when the mother is myself? To leave blame aside for the moment, let us try and divide these issues as my title divides them. First, desire.

Desire is never simply a private experience: feminist or not, we live in a relation to the socially constructed masculinity that has its base in men's relative public power. But I want here to look indoors and to suggest five elements in which I think a woman's heterosexual desire consists – some of these may be common to both sexes, others perhaps are not, and sexual experience is perhaps (thus far) the kind of information least easy to compare. What I shall not describe is anything about excitement or satisfaction: these are both too general and too particular to be relevant to my question.

The first element is something like aesthetic play – purposeless purposiveness: there is an aim but no end. The second is a recovery of childhood which consists in indulging the original polymorphous perversity, or whatever version of it you allow into adult consciousness: a special freedom in this regard that does not get experienced in other ways. It is what a woman friend of mine called being 'dirty,' but she meant a 'dirtiness' that is more or less the same as innocence. It is access to one's own body via the other's body.

The third element is something to do with nurturance. In Proust, the protagonist finds in his lover Albertine's kiss (however hopelessly his passion is based on a dialectic of contempt and evasiveness) a restored copy of the mother's goodnight kiss – a mixture of ceremony and habit on which as a child his security depended. This is a physical form of sustenance which has echoes of breastfeeding, whichever sex receives it from which.

Now something political: there is, I think, a pleasure in having power over the powerful. Any virgin, however repressed, sees the powerful effect her choices have on the desire of the man. Something of this is, I think, at the base of the pride taken by conventional women in having a son – temporarily in possession of a dependent phallus (as we are in another sense in bed), these mothers indulge in a combination of pride and contempt for the imitation man. The sexual version of this may be fleeting or symbolic, unless a sadomasochistic explicitness both aestheticizes and literalizes the power structure, but I think it exists in one form or other in every heterosexual encounter – not necessarily oppressively – for it remains also play and innocence. Another way of understanding such power-play as benign is to read it through the fifth element, which is narcissism. If a man in bed recovers the mother in one way – aggressively, perhaps, if he has never accepted the pains of separation – the woman recovers her in another. The mother is first love-object, first toy and world to both sexes. The woman in bed watching herself watched (is this what they mean by passivity?) is worshipping at the shrine of the mother via her own body; she both has and is.[2] The only similar moment of plenitude (and I have no idea if there is some similar moment for men) that I know of – but this latter is, strikingly, an *intellectual* plenitude, a plenitude of knowledge experienced via the body – is in pregnancy.

The man with whom the woman experiences this range of pleasures is, for her, sexy. If I have described this combination of elements as an experience of femininity, then by corollary the perception of these five potentials in the person of the lover is an experience of the masculine.

If desire is risk – love being the possibility of the impossible, the impossible being found to exist, now (in psychoanalytic terms, the achievement of the object) – then there is something in that plenitude of being that we could call phallic. It might be objected that of my list of five elements, only one – the political one – suggests a male object. It could also be objected that in the fifth element, the plenitude of narcissism, no other of either sex is needed – but this would not be so, since the narcissistic experience has to do with being *other to an other* for which sexuality is a necessary element (it is not the same with one's children). This otherness is sexual in that it proceeds from/produces gender difference.[3] By contrast, a woman's unsexual relationships with other women tend to be structured as a subject–subject encounter. Talking together, women create a weave of agreements. There is something more quarrelsome and differently self-conscious about heterosexual love, structured as it is both by the genderedness of desire and the social patterns of power. And by that very token, existentially if you like, the endorsement that comes from being desired by the other sex is uniquely risky and distinctively based on being his object. Heterosexual love can be (when it is what we wish it to be) a dangerously balanced endorsement via the position of object – object of his sentence, that is, not of his reification.

What then, if this need is a need of the masculine? Feminism exists to decenter the phallus as political instrument of magic – to argue for the danger and arbitrariness of that myth. Feminist marriage must decenter the power of the phallus in two crucial ways: in career equality and in equality of parenting. Both these equalities are based in the aim to make a home based on feminist values and 'women's skills.'

These two equalities are both practical and ideological: they appear in day-to-day choices (nights, rather, with breast or bottle, mornings waking to the radio-alarm not to lovemaking) but they represent our principles as they are embodied in economic reality. Here is the dilemma:

If we both want equal careers, where do we live? (And how rare any version of equality really is.) If one commutes – usually the man – the other is a single parent all week and at weekends they pass each other in the hall (this has been nicely termed a 'telegamous partnership'). Or her career, conventionally, lags some paces behind. Then what is she to do with her rightful anger, reproached by others as 'competitiveness'? If she lags behind, the phallus is in place all right in the household, as the fetish of power, even though it may embarrass them both.

As for equal parenting – suppose it is possible – do we reasonably define it by the dirtiness, the boringness and stressfulness of the work the father does? But if so, what about the fragrant bits – do we want to share those? Don't we insist after all (because this has something to do with our sexuality) on keeping for ourselves the passion between mother and child that begins at conception?

Feminist motherhood is woman-centered. How many of us have come to think we'd rather have women than men at the birth – not just holding the medical but the personal hand too? And not only because we have suspected they stop desiring us once they have seen this. Or how many of us have dreaded having sons because, as truly matrilinear women,[4] we carry our ideology as well as our desire in our wombs? What place is there in all this for a father?

In the mythology of patriarchal tradition, the mother is just the seedbed, the link in a chain that gives sons to fathers, passing on a name; the Oedipus complex, too, makes the 'desire of the mother' a temporary, childish stage. But feminism looks back to nature to rediscover that males have a minuscule and brief part in reproduction. And if we need women as friends, children to give us value, work to prove our creativity, what need is left for men? Simply to help provide a home and to give us the seed so that we can make and keep our children? But coming to this point, perhaps we are unintentionally reproducing an old pattern after all: if we keep men out of the center of parenthood it may be because we fear *but thereby make easier* their ability to separate from the family, consecrating their inessential place in it.

The phallus we need to become pregnant by is not the phallus of desire. Just short of expendable, it makes us culture's praying mantises. This is the man from whom we require work, not love. But we want to love him too . . .

Where does this leave his desire – that essential element in ours, if we are to be turned on by his otherness? Is the whole process inevitably going to take away his pride, and if it does will shame emasculate? Will he, left with the service side, become our wife? If we want him to nurture, provide and protect, are we feminizing him? If we are (and consider this a compliment, as we consider it for our sons – who wants a masculine boy?), then perhaps he can only in any case fail: for if we want women, we have our friends, and if our children want mothers, they have us.

And who are these good men? Are they the husbands we want because their parents have raised them repressively, to suffer, feel obligation and by the feminizing structures of guilt efface their wishes for the sake of the family? Can there be another way? If we insist that there can be new ways of being a good mother, for us now, do we allow them other ways of being a good father as well? For if we don't, then our sons will not know how to do it at all.

(Let me not be misunderstood – I am not arguing for the sexiness of *bad* men. I am assuming that the women I am thinking of will not have allied themselves with crass or unthinking men. The sexiness I have outlined is anything but macho, just as the goodness is the goodness of simple reason, however rare these qualities may be to find.)

How are our sons to become good men by day and sexy men at night? Can our husband push a supermarket trolley in the morning and turn us on twelve hours later? Must work preclude play? Will we inevitably move ever closer to a version of the invidious split men have made among women, with two possible results: either that my good man is your sexy man and vice versa, a tragi-comic chain with everyone facing two ways; or else two types of maleness are being produced, one good and one sexy.

If this split is really happening, a possible cause is this: over the centuries men have divided women into two types, building up Western culture on this unadmitted neurosis; now we have a little bit of power, very fragile and barely enjoyed, never self-justifying enough to go underground into psychosexual development – and with this insecure little bit of power we cannot (thank goodness) split the world but concentrate instead on our very small domestic/political patch.

Then we see the destructive result (and take the guilt on ourselves) in the husband who finds himself being a wife. We follow through the familiar logic that marriage is an institution which cannot support more than one whole person. If the man holds the reins (purse-strings, heartstrings) then sexuality is intact – someone is frustrated but no one is shamed. If it is the woman, if their time is her time, then something shocking is exposed, something neither men nor women can easily admit. The good man and the sexy man perhaps grow out of the two alternative structures – a depressing thought. If he wants to change from one mode to another, he will need to change beds. And then what happens?

Returning to the psychoanalytic angle, we might find another version of the cause. Let me propose that, rather than the phallus, the mother is the first whole object of desire. In the loving man of heterosexual desire (with whom we play, in whom we can see ourselves desirably reflected), do we find the mother who will exercise her power by lending us her phallus? Is our pleasure something to do with a moment of completeness thus entirely shared? But in that other man, the good husband, do we not take the phallus away to make our children, incorporating its virtue into a greater one? If so, we are refusing to let the plenitude be shared – no one may be mother but us.

Once again, can the man we choose for his genes also give pleasure? Can he continue to give pleasure? Can we be *la mère jouissante*? One reason why not might be that we have discovered pregnancy, childbirth, lactation and nurturing to be the real buzz. But it isn't *jouissance* because it isn't becoming the child again ourselves. Where is the space where our body can be at once sexual and maternal? Where is the space where the two men can be one man?

I return to the image of the son. We want to be something other than a momentary and despicable Jocasta. Look at a three-year-old (male or female), affectionate without guilt and happy in its body without vanity. Yes, they are already gendered at three, but need they grow into the split men and women of my title?

A year later the questions remain.[5] Looking at my generation of feminist women, I note the frequency of separation and divorce, telegamous partnerships being those (ironically, predictably) in which the split is effected with least scarring: for the children especially, the new structure of separate parenting runs on smoothly from the old. Wise heads nod at the inevitability of dual-career partnerships falling into separation, considering that was how they always were; we read in the failure of our monogamy and the success of our autonomy something both burdensome and pleasant – would we really rather be alone *without* the child-care demands that fill evenings, coupled with the 'free' weekends to catch up with everything else in a house where objects briefly stay where we put them? But we also reflect on the abandonment of a girlish hope that mature partnership might after all have been possible.

A few weeks ago I saw a film released from censorship after almost a decade: Nagisa Oshima's *Ai No Corrida* (*In the Realm of the Senses*) (1976). The intense and exclusive sexual passion of Kichi and Sada, which takes them indoors into an ever narrower private/artificial space heavily scented with their shared pleasure, ends in his slow strangulation by her followed by a careful castration that had most of the audience hiding their eyes. What was most seductive, and most unusual for a film portraying desire and violence in a heterosexual context, was the extent to which the man and his pleasure were the willing instrument of the woman's pleasure. As she strangles Kichi, Sada is co-opting his orgasm as her own (he, after all, dies as it happens); at the instant of his death, his phallus,[6] which hitherto she has borrowed in a mutual *jouissance*, becomes hers. We see the clothed body of Sada curved against the naked body of Kichi, he smiling peacefully, gashed red in the place where a woman is said to have 'no sex,' and carrying on his chest the avowal of their love that she has written with his blood, while the director's voice-over announces the historical facts: the original Sada wandered through Tokyo for four days with the severed genitals in her hands, 'radiantly happy,' and her case inspired a strange sympathy. Why is this woman happy with her lover's castrated remains? Why do the public and private systems of censure allow her both her passion and her gesture?

I recently spoke to a man who, after fifteen years of loving a woman at a distance, agreed enthusiastically to have a child with her saying he understood that, if he were to die, she wanted to have something (someone) that would keep the relationship incarnate. After changing his mind, he was appalled by her grief at the loss of that potential child, almost as if the now-broken promise was proved a mistake by the woman's transfer of bereavement from him to a child. Similarly, the logic of *Ai No Corrida* suggests that the woman cannot have both Kichi and his phallus; male-made and male-conceived, the film, of course, forms her wish out of his ambivalent wish, representing in his cheerful willingness a man's desire to be separated whole from part, and in her violence his wish to remain undivided. The relation of man to penis is one of peculiar mutual dependence; thus Freud, in a revealingly casual metonymy, refers to a boy as 'the small bearer of the penis' [*der kleine Penisträger*],[7] involuntarily evoking a kind of Obélix whose bearing is never done. What, in such a semi-joined pair, supports what, who depends on whom? If a man is (in his own phantasm, perhaps in ours) the metonym of a metonym, is castration not the logical desire and fear that motivates his relation to us?

If, at this drastic estimate, the lover is metonym to his metonym, servant to the phallus that may serve the woman better than himself, remaining finally in her body or her hands, are all men similarly dependent on, afraid of and *necessarily* separable from their children? Then, when they leave us, must they experience the shock of endorsing, in anger or gratitude, the proof of their voluntary redundancy now that they have left us with child? We know how nearly expendable the male is in sexual reproduction, how entirely redundant in the thousands of species that reproduce asexually, how, to rephrase Samuel Butler, a man is simply a woman's way of making another woman.[8] A male lion entering a pride consisting of females and young will clear the decks for the greatest reproduction of his genes by killing the cubs and causing abortion in any pregnant female. Unlike lions, human men can be deeply attached to their children, loving them in a passionate responsible way indistinguishable from the mother's way, except that they go and we stay.

Are there, finally, as Irigaray and Cixous suggest, two economies, one tendentiously tied to the masculine, the other to the feminine? The first, an economics of scarcity, reasons by either/or, by separation, competition and jealousy: it institutes the harem and *gynaeceum*, adultery as the normal mode of passion, the womb unable to hold both child and man at once, and culture as a great *trompe l'oeil* that imitates our reproduction, assigning it to nature, dividing us from other, conscious creativities and turning our blood magic into scarlet letters.[9] The second is an economics of plenty, a logic of both/and, passing beyond both Romanticism and Freudianism; by this latter reasoning, more demand produces more supply and there is, I should like to argue, nothing intrinsically feminine or even gendered in it (though indeed its contrary is clearly patriarchal). Its mode can be seen reflected in the two least bloody of secretions, breast-milk and semen, both of which are supplied more generously as demand increases in strength or frequency. But nowadays we are rightly fearful of mixing body fluids; by reason of death, our heterosexuality has lost its traditional tie to penetration, and the surface becomes the place where pleasure ought instead to be written. What I have spoken of in this paper is the question of an internal event (love, gestation, the doubly desiring womb, the moment of shared pleasure) turning into an external one (marriage, politics, the separable phallus, the once-born child). Intimacy is surely something to do with a penetration without violence, cutting off neither the inside nor the outside. Can the economics of plenty allow a combination, against the constraints of our bad old habits, of male and female, lovers and parents, good and sexy?

NOTES

1 See Dorothy Dinnerstein, *The Mermaid and the Minotaur* (published in the UK as *The Rocking of the Cradle and the Ruling of the World*), New York: Harper and Row, 1977; London: The Women's Press, 1978. The feminist literature on motherhood is massive and speedily increasing. Most influential, though very different, are, on the one hand, Dinnerstein and Nancy Chodorow, *The Reproduction of Mothering*, Berkeley: University of California Press, 1978; and on the other, the work of French theorists such as Julia Kristeva, Hélène Cixous and Luce Irigaray. For useful recent summaries of changing views on motherhood in the last thirty years of feminism, see Lynne Segal, *Is the Future Female?* London: Virago, 1987; Marianne Hirsch, *The Mother-Daughter Plot*, Bloomington: University of Indiana Press, 1989; and my own entry on 'Motherhood' in ed. Elizabeth Wright *et al.*, *Psychoanalysis and Feminism: A Critical Dictionary*, Oxford: Blackwell, forthcoming.

2 See Dinnerstein, Women's Press edition, pp. 61–63.

3 I use the term 'gender' here to refer to a subject/object difference leaning on an axis of desire and power, whether or not the two subjects in the encounter (ideally a seesaw structure of balance and exchange) are sexed differently, male and female. Genet's male homosexuals are, in this sense, sharply distinguished by gender – even if such gendering may occasionally be reversible, his most muscular thugs carrying such delicious names as 'Mignon-les-Petits-Pieds' and 'Notre-Dame-des-Fleurs.'

4 For a development of this term, see my *The Adulteress's Child*, Cambridge: Polity, forthcoming, especially the introduction.

5 The following remarks are borrowed from the Conclusion of *The Adulteress's Child*.

6 I am using the term 'phallus' in this section with a shameless lack of reference to Lacan. What I have in mind is the already sufficiently phantasmatic organ attached to the body of a male lover making love.

7 Sigmund Freud, 'The Dissolution of the Oedipus Complex' (1924), *The Pelican Freud Library*, vol. 7, Harmondsworth: Penguin, 1977, p. 321.

8 The original ('it has, I believe, been often remarked that a hen is only an egg's way of making another egg') is from Samuel Butler, *Life and Habit* (Trübner, London, 1878), p. 134; it is quoted in Jeremy Cherfas and John Gribbin, *The Redundant Male*, London: Bodley Head, 1984, p. 11. I am indebted to them also for the attractive formula: 'Males are simply modified females tailored to a particular role in the reproductive process' (54). Their book is, however, a slide from an excitingly modest title to a grotesquely sociobiologized analysis: in the chapter where they finally speak of human women, one might think culture had never existed. For a more useful presentation of the facts and arguments from nature, see Sarah Blaffer Hrdy, *The Woman who Never Evolved*, Cambridge, Mass.: Harvard University Press, 1981;

and Irene Elia, *The Female Animal*, Oxford: Oxford University Press, 1985.

9 See ed. Thomas Buckley and Alma Gottlieb, *Blood Magic*, Berkeley: University of California Press, 1988, and especially the wonderful Chris Knight, 'Menstrual Synchrony and the Australian Rainbow Snake,' pp. 232–55.

Chapter 3

Men and women
The use and abuse of mutual space

Andrea Spurling

THE PROBLEM

In 1988, King's College, Cambridge initiated a research project to identify obstacles to the full development of women's academic careers at Cambridge University.[1] One of the problems identified during fieldwork was usually articulated as a conflict between men and women in the use of 'space' – whether this be time in mixed learning groups or space in the College bar. Complaints by students described women being 'squeezed out' of tutorial discussion by men, and this was confirmed by academic supervisors' comments. Commonly, this process of elimination initially involved women being denied time to speak, but the result was often that they ultimately absented themselves voluntarily either by keeping silent, or staying away.

THE VALUES OF SILENCE

This paper considers the quality and use of spaces, whether they are physical areas or periods of time, for it is in the use of such space that people's spirits can either flourish or be trampled to death. Art is the medium of the spirit, and artists know that space doesn't have to be visually or aurally occupied to be engaged. In works of art space is powerfully activated. There is a qualitative relationship between adjacent areas or periods, the *inhabited* quality of the one and the *uninhabited* quality of the other mutually emphasizing one another. Sculptors and potters literally embody the flow of space that is both enclosed by, and that encloses, their work. Even massive pieces contain space trapped within their material, whether it be open- or close-grained. In the hands of sculptors such as Henry Moore space is so potent that it pierces and fragments granite itself. Dancers and actors move through space and time across a stage. The dimensions of the actual stage stay the same, but the movements define the quality of imagined spaces, those surrounding the dancer, and those created in the minds of the audience: vast or cramped; friendly or hostile; crowded or deserted. Architects, like sculptors on a giant scale, control the interaction of solids, volumes and spaces, and involve people's lives in the process. The great lawns of the Cambridge colleges define areas into which pressured minds can expand and find space for maneuver. They provide uninterrupted expanses, overlooked by rooms where selected people tussle with problems and ideas. Coincidentally or otherwise, the lawns also reflect different kinds of space elsewhere, for in an overcrowded city they indicate the possession of wealth. The lawns symbolize money in accounts where others have only a void.

Silence is as potent as space, and just as space can fracture stone so can silence overpower the human imagination. (It was *'le silence éternel de ces espaces infinis'* that terrified Pascal.)[2] The structure of music is essentially the formal or fortuitous management of sounds and silences over a period, and just as the visual arts articulate space, so music articulates silence. The difference between an exciting and a facile performance rests in the management of silence, whether or not it is written in by the composer. Similarly, the measure of an actor is not so much the *how* as the *when*: the timing of the delivery of the words. Silence focuses attention, places stress, on what went before and what comes after.

The management of silence is essential to the craft of directing learning groups because silence is an aspect of the mutual space through which the members can communicate. To obliterate silence is to ignore a vital medium of communication. It is the first speaker, usually the tutor,[3] who establishes the mode of interaction for the group. The mode of the tutorial needs to be made clear – whether it will take the form of a discussion or an enquiry. Students need to know whether they are expected to serve up what they know and take sides in an argument, or to enquire into what they don't and cooperate in the attempt. A discussion sets up the mutual space as a competitive platform for displays of knowledge; an enquiry implies a cooperative space in which to listen, think, and pool ideas. It is not surprising if there is a conflict of interests when some people in a group behave as if silence is empty while others feel it is engaged.

SILENCE AND THE SOCRATIC METHOD

A discussion is the examination of a question by arguments for and against. At Cambridge, 'Discussions' play an important role in the formal proceedings of the University, and the relevant polemical skills are highly valued. The conventional form is analytical and logical, and it is no coincidence that this is the form that also prevails in the British legal and parliamentary systems. Many Oxbridge graduates ultimately enter these systems, where they enjoy considerable success. The origin of this convention is the teaching method known as 'Socratic dialogue,' based on a sequence of questions and answers by which the tutor leads the student towards a greater awareness of existing knowledge. The endpoint of the process is known in advance, and the questions indicate the route to the answers. The method provides a way of guiding students through unfamiliar territory or a particular syllabus, as well as teaching intellectual discipline. When the subject of tutorial discussion is an essay written by a student, the author has to defend the thesis of his or her argument in the face of critical questioning by the tutor and other members of the group. The aim here is to encourage 'intellectual rigour,' meaning absolute accuracy and meticulous thoroughness in the examination of a thesis. But 'rigour' also has connotations of *harshness, severity*, and, formerly, *rigidity*.[4] The Socratic method leads to close examination, but strictly according to the sequence of rational argument. Rationality as a methodological basis has the authority of classicism in the culture of Western Europe, but that does not necessarily make it the best method by which to examine, for example, the psychological or social workings of that very culture. Socratic dialogue is also a method that places learning groups in a context of combat and defence, effectively setting the tutor against the student, and one 'partner' in a tutorial in competition with another. For those who understand the convention, and who are robust enough to survive cross-examination, it can encourage the development of quick thinking and the verbal skills of presentation in the face of criticism. But intelligent people come from backgrounds of varying conventions, some of which may be characterized more by sensitivity than by robustness. Argument can also distort the relevant importance of performance and attack compared with the actual processes of thinking. It focuses on contention: the initial question sets up the expectation of an answer, and the one who gets in first and hangs onto the space while working out an answer has the best chance of getting the crown of laurels – there is no reward for hanging back.

It was clear from the King's College research project that this performance is something that, by and large, male students had learned to do in secondary school but many women had not. The effect of this difference was threefold. First, the women assumed that because the men were more ready to jump in with an answer they were intellectually more able. This assumption, in turn, undermined the women's confidence in their own ability, because they found that they were still thinking about the question while the men were already – apparently – answering it. Finally, if they lasted in a group long enough to realize that the men didn't necessarily have the answer, but were just 'hogging the space' in the hope they'd find it while they were talking, the women became resentful. It was not actually that the men could think more quickly than the women, but that they had learnt the rules of the game, and knew the value of saying *anything* in order to stake their claim to discussion space. They were prepared, if necessary, to risk coherence in the early stages of the process, before they had reached a conclusion in their thinking. Men were also more likely to use the amplified rhetoric of public utterance, which is characterized by devices such as double negatives and repetition of the subject by name. This both slows down the delivery of ideas and artificially inflates the content. Women students and academics alike commented on the way that male students more often than their female colleagues seemed happy 'to talk absolute rubbish.' If this tutorial method produces people who can think on their feet in a crisis, it also produces its share of pompous windbags, for in this kind of argument there is no room for silence.

PENETRATING ARGUMENT

One aim of higher education is the development of perceptive intelligence, the kind that can identify and enter the very heart of a problem. The ideal is described as a 'penetrating mind,' and the penetrative imagery is echoed in the notion of a 'rapier wit.' The combination of these two represented an ideal for university undergraduates for centuries – as the Oxford Union, Houses of Parliament, courts of law, and thousands of after-dinner speeches bear (often unkind) witness. It is above all a quintessentially masculine creation. At Cambridge signs of its continued existence are still evident, and echoes of its ringing tones still pierce the air. Penetration is its behavioral mode, whether it be 'plumbing the depths' of a problem or impaling an opponent on the 'point' of argument. 'Brilliance' is used to convey the idea of striking ability; something diamond-like that fascinates but which is simultaneously rock-hard, with a cutting edge.

There may not be a consciously aggressive intent behind the exercise of intellectual skill through argument, but people caught up in its process can feel exposed and vulnerable, especially if they are strangers to its culture. (It is now recognized in Britain that rape victims may be reluctant to appear in court for the prosecution because cross-examination recreates too vividly the experience of physical violation.) Some women respondents in the King's College research described feelings of 'harassment' and 'vulnerability' in tutorials. Not surprisingly, such feelings and the 'learning' environments with which they were associated had tended to undermine, rather than to increase, their self-confidence.

In sexual intercourse, 'penetration' is a technical term relevant to everything from seduction to rape, and the situation is not dissimilar in verbal intercourse. The ultimate effect is not so much in the technical act as in the manner in which it is carried out. Among some feminists (women and men), 'penetration' is used as if it is automatically synonymous with domination. Some women feel out of place in a traditional tutorial setting because they experience Socratic argument as too masculine, both as a process to be subject to and to use. The 'orgasmic tutorial,' identified during the colloquium that gave rise to this paper, is the kind that encourages and rewards intrusive, competitive behavior and an impressive climax of reasoning. In this context, the person with the greatest potency is less the one who possesses knowledge than the one who makes the greatest display of it. Not all men choose to behave in this way, and not all women object to it. Although respondents to the research project expressed the problem in terms of men and women, it actually resides more in the gender of academic conventions. The challenge is to find alternative modes that suit people who work best in less masculine, non-combative styles, whether they are women or men.

ENQUIRY AS PEDAGOGICAL METHOD

An alternative to discussion as a tutorial mode is enquiry, which is the pursuit of understanding through essentially open-ended questions, rather than the closed form of Socratic dialogue. As this approach focuses more on the identification and development of ideas than on the persuasive presentation of knowledge, group enquiry may well lead to periods of silence when people are actively thinking. Such a mode involves, essentially, the sharing of ideas and skills – using them in common, rather than trying to impress or outperform other members of the group. The common experience provides an opportunity for the development of skills of thinking, as well as of articulation. Learning to think creatively as a member of a group necessitates the development of sensitivity to others and to the quality of the 'mutual space.' The personal and group skills it encourages are of value in and beyond higher education, and not only in the fields of legal and political power. It develops habits of imaginative involvement and intellectual flexibility and, above all, social skills that have greater creative potential than the competitive framework of argument. It is not necessarily the best form of teaching for all subjects at all times, any more than is discussion. Some subjects, such as mathematics and physics, have a high 'content base' which might be better learned with the aid of computers. The method needs to be appropriate to the task.

When *the skills of intellectual enquiry* are the focus of learning groups, people can be encouraged to articulate the questions that identify and open up possible routes to understanding. Students need to develop sufficient confidence to present unfinished thoughts, which might have potential but which might equally prove to be dead-ends, and they are likely to need help in this. They need a supportive learning environment; educational methods based on competition and challenge are more likely to inhibit the development of such confidence than to encourage it, and are likely to convey the message that answers are more highly valued than questions.

Perhaps the suckling of an infant is the best model of physical intimacy for the supportive teaching method. Like intercourse, it involves the interpenetration of body spaces, but it is rarely seen as 'domination,' and competition is not normally part of an act that both satisfies and nourishes.

MUTUAL SPACE

Male hormones do not endow people with superior intellectual ability any more than female hormones encumber others with irreversible psychological obstacles. If men tend to gain better examination results and have greater professional success than women in traditional universities, as they do, that is because the conventions and structures of those institutions were designed to reward masculine behavior, and they have not changed since the days when academics and students were exclusively male. Whether in working groups or in personal relationships, the space between people can only be made truly mutual by emasculating some of the existing conventions. As long as feminization remains associated mainly with the reduction of power, it has, for many people, little attraction. The problem of power, like space, is learning how to share it.

NOTES

1 Andrea Spurling, *Report of the Women in Higher Education Research Project*, King's College, Cambridge, 1990. The project was run as a program of action research, and the research report includes details of the background and methodology of the project, and of the College's immediate response. Copies are available from: The Secretary, King's College Research Centre, King's College, Cambridge CB2 lST. Price at the time of going to press: £15.00.

2 Pascal, *Pensées*, ed. Brunschvicg, Paris: Hachette, 1909, i.19.

3 To avoid repetition, 'tutor' will be used throughout to refer to the leader of a learning group. Tutorials are known as 'supervisions' at Cambridge. They are ideally one-to-one, but very often involve two or three students.

4 'Rigour,' *Collins Dictionary of the English Language*, 1986 ed.

Recommended reading

Brittan, Arthur (1989) *Masculinity and Power*, Oxford, Basil Blackwell.
Thomas, Kim (1990) *Gender and Subject in Higher Education*, Buckingham, Open University Press.

Part II

Writing between the lines

Chapter 4

Men after feminism
Sexual politics twenty years on

Joseph Bristow

MISSING MEN

Twenty years on, after two decades of feminist struggle, you might imagine that men, as well as women, had learned some lessons from the findings of one of the founding texts of the Women's Liberation Movement (WLM): Kate Millett's world-wide bestseller, *Sexual Politics* (1969). It almost goes without saying that for all that time it has been an exceptionally influential book. In feminist literary criticism, Millett's tome captures the atmosphere of what was right and what was wrong with radical feminism at its inception. The book has all the gusto of the Civil Rights Movement animating every page. Undoubtedly a monument to the rapid changes in consciousness that took place in the late sixties, it helped to bring the idea of sexual equality proudly out of the closet. (The metaphor is intentional; its year of publication coincided with the Stonewall riots in the gay bars of New York City.) *Sexual Politics*, perhaps the most notorious doctoral thesis in literature ever to go into paperback, has always been a source of controversy, and it is not my intention here to repeat all the points made so trenchantly by Cora Kaplan in her exacting résumé of its salient contradictions.[1] Rather, Millett's amorphous, ambitious, and, to say the least, highly memorable account of phallocratic power will simply serve me here as a starting-point for thinking through how and why within feminism her uncompromising analysis of unrelenting misogyny both opened up, and almost simultaneously closed down, the analysis of the problem of men in Western culture. Indeed, the book attends to different masculinities – both straight and gay – in a way that, one might think, would have served as an inspiration for all ensuing critiques. *Sexual Politics*, however, is probably recalled more for its theoretical flaws than its thoughtfulness about men.

As far as subsequent feminist criticism is concerned, perhaps Millett's cardinal achievement was her presentation of 'sexual politics' as a term for understanding that power was brutally gendered, and that men, to disastrous effects, were the bearers of it. Fictional narratives, by loathsome male chauvinist pigs (or MCPs), made this patently clear. But, in retrospect, Millett's idea of 'sexual politics' is startlingly different from what it has come to mean now. Indeed, it would seem that, given the range and scope of current debates about pleasure, desire, identity, and difference, the term 'sexual politics' is only too visibly split down the middle. The sexualization of politics and the politicization of sex are not, in this peculiar chiasmus, quite the same thing any more. Two decades have brought an avalanche of feminist theories, productively, if at times antagonistically, moving in diverse directions, so that the WLM and the MCP are acronyms left behind in a somewhat distant past. But what consequences, I wonder, has feminist theory – perhaps the most exciting corpus of scholarship around – had for all the potential MCPs who have grown up in its wake? Here, in thinking about sexual politics, I am thinking about a problem that still lingers all these years on. This is the possibility of a sexual politics for (straight-identified) men, a sexual politics that has failed to emerge even from those studies which ostensibly take it as their object of enquiry (notoriously, *Men in Feminism* [1987], of which more later).

These days 'gender studies' reaches very high levels of sophistication. Publishers' lists testify to the extraordinary accomplishments of the multiplicity of feminisms. Yet it is sometimes difficult to see quite where a common feminist politics is precisely located. Endlessly refining how we (that is, as sexually/politically conscious subjects) might speak of sex, gender, and sexuality, those of us who pride ourselves on a self-reflexive deconstructive turn of mind may have so many ways of talking about politics and sex (or sex and politics: choose your order) that the thought of any change in the immediate future may seem utterly immobilizing. Moreover, the climate of 'difference' has led not so much towards celebratory heterogeneity but more towards expressly divided opinions. In a world where obstacle-making sectarianism frequently has full rein, there is simply such a range of considerations to make that it is sometimes hard – with this surplus of theory to hand – to get any one sexual–political priority in place. At the moment, with various camps lining up along the divisions of essentialism versus constructionism within, noticeably, lesbian, gay, black and women's communities (and even the idea of community is under regular scrutiny: embraced and demythologized at once), it would often appear that dissension outweighs agreement. Currently, in Britain, one of the main polarizations of debate concerns the banning and freeing up of pornography – the Campaign against Pornography and Censorship (CPC: a Dworkin/MacKinnon derivative) is embattled against Feminists against Censorship (FAC), a group linked, in some ways, to the predominantly libertarian politics of *Feminist Review*. It is worth bearing in mind that one of the reasons why Millett's extraordinary book was, and remains, such an engaging read is that it had, most definitively, a subject on which it could polemicize, and a target that the majority of feminists could agree upon. It is, in its own terms, a very straightforward account of phallocentric culture with fiction, a transparent medium, directly communicating the sins of the fathers. These days, with our subjectivities fading, unable to constitute themselves quite as fully as we might like, and with the general erosion of democratic socialist values fostered by the 1980s (Reagan, Thatcher), it is altogether less clear how we might take our sexual futures into our hands.

Well before the troubling uncertainties of postmodernity became clear to us, Millett in the late sixties had a definite sexual–political program in place: to critique the long-standing misogyny of the patriarchy which the postwar period had made altogether more visible than ever before. Collapsing any discernible differences between, say, Sigmund Freud and Henry Miller, her sequence of chapters boiled down to much the same thing: that these masculinist texts sought to depose, degrade, repress, and ultimately destroy women. But, interestingly, few – feminists or radical men – followed her along the same path. It is with these thoughts in mind – about Millett's sense of direction and our sense of dispersal – that I'll move on to consider some of the main questions in the hardly novel men and feminism debate. My base here will be literary studies, since that is the area in which I work, and where – as I'll outline later – one of my main (male) identities is located, and that is my teaching identity. What I want to do here is shift the discussion about men 'in/and/or' feminism towards some practical considerations about how straight-identified men might, in an institutional context, become a little more self-critical about the power they bear.

My interests, to repeat, lie with the absence – a conspicuous (some might say diminishing) absence – of a radical male sexual politics in the wake of 1968. Although men's groups have been formed, and anti-masculinist journals, such as *Changing Men* (US) and *Achilles Heel* (UK), have been in production for some time, and although there has, of course, been a gay men's movement (and a substantial body of theory and practice emerging from it), straight-identified men – one of the main objects for transformation by and through feminist and gay critique – are still largely without a vocabulary for articulating a radical difference within the sex/gender hierarchy. In literary criticism, all too noticeably, there is little discernible movement by men to situate, analyze, and realize historical changes in the masculinities represented in the texts (often male ones) set before them. Although theories of masculinity might suggest that maleness is predicated upon an unbending resistance to change, men, undeniably, have been changing (even if not self-consciously) through the centuries – but rarely, it might seem, for the better. What I want to do here is examine some theoretical and practical implications in thinking and writing about men 'after' feminism. The preposition labors on a purposive pun. The men in question are those who have come (historically) 'after' feminism, and then men who are politically 'after' (in search of, desiring) a 'feminism' of their own.

THE HOMOSOCIAL CONTRACT

Ever since Millett opened *Sexual Politics* with several appallingly sexist quotations from Henry Miller's hyper-horny *Tropic of Cancer* (1949), trends within feminist literary analysis have been driven a long way from this and the other pornutopic escapades to be found in Norman Mailer and D.H. Lawrence – whom, incidentally, Millett manages not only glaringly to misread but also, more perversely, for whom she shows a rather grudging respect (Kaplan says, wryly, that Millett treats her male protagonists as if they were 'confessed criminals').[2] It was left to Juliet Mitchell, in 1974, to correct Millett's infamous account of penis envy, thus opening up the very complex dialogues that have ensued between Freudian psychoanalysis and feminism to uncover what 'femininity' may have represented for Freud in all its problematic reinscriptions in his work.[3] Only recently have theories and histories of masculinity entered into debates about 'gender' – a term which sometimes appears currently to function as a euphemism for women and/or feminism. (There does not, yet again, seem to be a body of adequate theory by men on 'gender.' So, once more, men are more often than not implicated in, while not participating in, the conundrums of this topic.) Since its publication, *Sexual Politics*, with its clear (but not exclusive) emphasis on men's writing, has, in fact, remained something of an anomaly. This is not to say that feminist critics have not engaged with masculinity (that would be nonsense), but it has hardly been among feminist criticism's long list of priorities. In any case, if masculinity is a man's problem (which, undoubtedly, it is) then perhaps men should be left to get on with doing something about it? That is the perfectly reasonable assumption on which a great deal of feminist enquiry would seem to subsist.

That said, Millett's book, if analyzing men, was not exactly dealing with masculinity. Her thesis was about patriarchy: an object of enquiry which has of necessity continued to feature centrally in feminist analysis. The trouble is that patriarchy describes not 'gender' as such but a material structure. Patriarchy pertains to the gendered regulation of production and re-production, and, in the course of detailing the mechanisms – especially the institutions – through and in which men maintain power, the analysis of patriarchy seems, to this day, to leave masculinity behind as the uninterrogated premise upon which it may proceed. Circa 1969, the realm of patriarchy, it would seem, contained two clear-cut classes of men: male chauvinist pigs, on the one hand, and homosexuals (plus John Stuart Mill, a sort of traitor to his sex) on the other. Placing them thus side by side, Millett drew one startling conclusion. In one shocking quotation after another, it appeared that Mailer, Lawrence, and the Nazis were really 'repressed homosexuals,' as the example of Genet was there to prove (a whole chapter is given over to him). In Millett's divide-and-rule world of moral oppositions between men, straight was bad, and gay was good. But it has become much clearer in the past two decades that object-choice does not necessarily orientate one's politics (even if, ideally, it should do). In any case, Millett's 'repressed homosexuality' hypothesis has some alarming implications – in fact, it has an appallingly homophobic equation at its centre. To assert that arch-patriarchs are basically homosexual is to suggest that male homosexuality is the root of all misogyny. In this epoch of AIDS, gay male sexuality often comes to symbolize – at different levels within the popular imagination – either a turning away from women, or a plain hatred of them. (Symptoms of this view can be detected in some zones of feminist criticism.)[4] A desire for the same sex, of course, does not mean the rejection of the different. Besides, whether we are reading Freud or Foucault, we know that sameness and difference are, wherever gender is concerned, hard to separate out from one another – to the point, perhaps, that the opposition has by now become logically unmanageable.

The tortured mental acrobatics of the same-but-different paradigm emerges very usefully in the one book which has made the most significant steps in shifting the debate about masculinity in recent years. It is also a book which has, lest we forget it, made important new alignments between feminism and gay male politics. The work in question, of course, is Eve Kosofsky Sedgwick's *Between Men* (1985).[5] It is a study rightly held in high regard, and its by now well-known arguments are worth restating, especially as they are sometimes provocatively fuzzy at the edges. This book, which examines an unexpected assortment of canonical literary works, opens with an account of the 'homosocial continuum': a vague but usable term, considerably modified from Adrienne Rich's work,[6] it serves to describe varieties of male-to-male relations. Sedgwick notes that there are precarious calibrations marked along this slipping and sliding scale. Her readings of plays, poems, and fictions attempt to indicate how and why in the nineteenth century a more decisive break between 'homosexual' and 'homosocial' relations began to open up, working together with increasingly virulent forms of homophobia.

Although Sedgwick's use of historical materials is sketchy, her theoretical outline has, to say the least, been influential. There are several basic and by now familiar points that need to be noted in Sedgwick's discussion. First of all, she claims that forms of male bonding are not necessarily based on the 'repressed homosexuality' hypothesis (vulgarized from Freud and expounded by Millett) – with all its damaging insinuations. Instead, she proposes that genital contact between men is policed by forms of regulated homophobia that demonstrate how difficult it is to maintain either a straight or a gay identity – both psychically and politically. But homophobia is not the only regulative mechanism marked along the 'homosocial.' The 'homosocial' also establishes its cohesiveness through the 'traffic of women' – a system of exchange theorized within Lévi-Strauss's structural anthropology (rerouted through Gayle Rubin's classic essay of 1975).[7] These, then, are the key issues at stake.

It is easy to find fault with Sedgwick's path-breaking theorizing. For a start, it would seem to produce the sociality of which it speaks without any clear reference to psychical realities, thus obscuring how and why identifications are drawn up on either side of the 'homosocial'/homosexual divide. Although Sedgwick's thesis is that both sides of this asymmetry are already implied in one another, it is nonetheless impossible to comprehend why men end up on some points of the scale, and not others. In other words, the 'homosocial' does not account for why some guys turn out to be part of the dominant, and why others end up lodged in a deviant zone within that dominant. This question of absent case histories aside (the absence of psychoanalysis would appear to be completely deliberate), there have, as is usual with an influential book, been several critiques of other aspects of *Between Men* and Sedgwick's numerous subsequent essays. For instance, some have complained about how her conceptualization of the 'traffic in women' as points of exchange lending cohesion to the 'homosocial continuum' excludes any notion of lesbian desire. This would seem to be a valuable objection since Rich's imprecise idea of a 'lesbian continuum' necessarily works from a different base from that of male 'homosociality.' Rich places the socially subordinated femininity as the prior term of woman-to-woman relations: lesbianism is Rich's foundation for considering femininity. Sedgwick's 'homosocial' scale, by contrast, has male homosexuality tucked inside it, as (apparently) an implied support or supplement for male heterosexuality, itself constituted by homophobia and misogyny. Male 'homosociality,' in other words, may be interpreted here as an overarching structure of male sexual phobias, requiring while reviling genital contact with both women and men. Taken to theoretical (if not practical) extremes, the 'homosocial' leaves no space for a positive male heterosexuality. At the same time, it reminds us of a largely abominated male homosexuality. Male sexuality, then, wherever it is located within the 'homosocial,' remains either the subject or object of phobia. This violent sociality seems to make heterosexual men fear one another because they are in danger of becoming homosexual.

There are further problems that need to be dealt with here. Although, in Sedgwick's theory, male heterosexuality may manifest itself as the ultimate in sexual pathology (and this is where straight-identified men may start to object), the 'homosocial continuum' has been upheld as a model with a dangerously implicated homophobia all of its own. This point has been brought up in a depressing debate between Sedgwick and one of her closest, and most ungenerous, readers, David van Leer in *Critical Inquiry*.[8] Van Leer rather unhelpfully indicates how Sedgwick, as a feminist, does not have the privilege – or inside knowledge or entitlement – to comprehend gay male sexuality, and that her work accidentally pathologizes gay manhood because it constructs male homosexuality as a structure of panic within the 'homosocial continuum.' (It is a 'panic' because, for those men walled up inside the closet, homosexuality is always on the cliff-teetering verge of being let out.) This critical debate is interesting in so far as it delineates the phobic boundaries that can settle around disputes between gay men and feminists – with imputed misogyny, on the one side, and implied homophobia, on the other. I take this as an example of a singularly paralyzing manifestation of current sexual politics. Van Leer accentuates the importance of addressing gay politics from a position of privilege (or authenticity) within the gay community. Such an argument vouches for a voice of truth (one of political if not 'sexualized' correctness) to underwrite the proprieties or improprieties of a gay critique. This is a monopolizing way of excluding, in particular, feminist theorists, like Sedgwick, from creating a politics of alliances – a politics which must attempt to balance the need for subcultural groups to work together with an understanding that we live in an inevitably (subculturally) divided culture. If we take it that Sedgwick was trying, almost single-handedly, to create a politics from which masculinity could be rethought, and then remade (for all women and men) from a feminist position, then there are somewhat more positive ways of using her work to investigate even more closely the homosocial contract – wherein men decide (at whatever levels of consciousness) to take up a place along the male scale. We need to proceed from her analysis to develop a historical and political understanding of the process by which men acquire certain (different) positions across the very wide gamut of 'homo' (similar) interests in one another.

THE WRITING ON THE WALL

Highly appropriate examples of the curious and contradictory inscriptions that demarcate the 'homosocial continuum,' and examples which deserve a lot of ethnographic fieldwork, are the writings on the walls of men's bathrooms. (Innovative work in this arena is especially important for research in and around HIV/AIDS – where many professionals in the field now make a point of talking not so much about gay, straight, or bisexual men, but more about 'men who have sex with men': it is a significant, because much more elastic, distinction.) Although bathroom graffiti varies from one context to another – the scrawls on the walls of one's workplace are not going to be entirely congruent with those scribblings marked up in a railway station – there are, and I think this is crucial, strong links between them. In any case, graffiti in cubicles is shaped by generic conventions – notably the misogynistic content of a very crude kind of epigrammatic wit. Not all men, by the way, participate in this unique form of collaborative male writing. Some of us are compelled to sit there and simply read. Let me, then, digress slightly, lower the lavatory seat (and, no doubt, lower the tone), and take a look at some of the things we routinely find there. Lavatory walls do not conform to one type, and their spatial layout can be strikingly different from one place to another (France and Britain make a stark contrast). There are those, for example, which are scrubbed clean like a palimpsest (marking out a war between the authorities and the scribes), and those which bear the competing inscriptions of several years, so the lavatory wall analyzed here will necessarily be one made up from bits and pieces of writing I've observed whenever and wherever nature has called. It is loosely representative of what any man might stumble on in either a railway station or a workplace in Britain. This imaginary men's room, most definitely, is a significant nodal point along the seemingly diverse interests of the 'homosocial continuum.' It is where secrets are shared in private, and forms of male sexual identity confirmed, and it is where *agents provocateurs* from the police force make countless successful arrests against 'cottaging' or 'tea-room trade' – sexual 'trade,' that is, between many men who would never identify themselves in public as homosexual, let alone as gay. This, the literal closet of mind and body, is where the homophobe throws in his lot with the homosexual – by various roundabout but telling twists and turns. In among the pornographic cartoons (anuses, penises, and vaginas – all rather exaggerated in size), the swastikas (celebrating the ultimate gentlemen's club), and the British National Front acronym ('NF': the clearest sign of white male supremacism), there are the names of rival football teams (boys supporting boys), supposed contact numbers for prostitutes (presumably, the name of his own or his friend's girlfriend), and various declarations about sexual exploits (a narrative of highly unlikely stories, both heterosexual and homosexual). Here, as the orifices open, and the pen makes its mark on this sexual bulletin board, men try to make sexual contact with other men, giving times, dates, and, sometimes, desired size and age. Against these assignations, the football supporter turns his hand away from the player of his dreams, draws an arrow, and pins down the homosexual with violent abuse. At times, there is a radical dialogy between these sparring-partners – where a whole section of wall is given over to an exchange of insults. Here, indeed, is one of the few places where men – who may identify themselves in completely different ways – are, behind closed doors, usually singly but at times in pairs, attempting to talk to one another. The point I'm making, of course, is that they probably have a lot more in common than they may care to think (or even admit). All these men want something from men. And that wanting – in this lavatorial space, momentarily isolated from the social – is articulated in here in a manner that we are unlikely to find anywhere else in the world. This closet – the most openly anonymous of places – traverses the distinction between public and private that still places strategic *cordons sanitaires* around class and gender (although, it has to be said, British 'public conveniences' are frequently unhygienic: the dirty body/dirty talk link is important here – but it would take up another paper to think it through).

To comprehend the writing on the wall, and perhaps to make some steps to lessen its violence (between men and towards women), a couple of things might be done within the groves of academe. Literary studies could, to begin with, reopen the debate about the malenesses to be found, page after page, in practically every text we have to handle. To strengthen our knowledge of these men – and to get somewhat closer to a notion of 'male reading' – detailed histories of masculinity are needed. For the moment, I'll leave the question of 'male reading' to one side. Let me make one or two remarks first about how I have approached the question of writing a small-scale cultural history of Victorian men. I have not, I should add, been writing about the history of men's room graffiti.

My own recent work has attempted to trace a pattern in homosocial relations in 'boys' own' literature (from the penny dreadfuls [of the 1860s and 1870s] to Robert Louis Stevenson's *Treasure Island* [1883]). Although the book I recently completed, *Empire Boys*, ranges widely across debates about literacy and British foreign policy, it has at its center a concern with how and why a particularly combative masculinity came into its own in the 1870s and 1880s when the respectable boys' weeklies were on the ascendant.[9] Identifying historical breaks in the homosocial continuum is inevitably complex, given the seemingly infinite number of social forces exerting pressure on one's object of investigation. Yet it is becoming clearer to me that a strategic ban on 'manly friendship' – the type espoused by Christian Socialism of the 1850s – was established at the point when, in the 1870s, more and more middle-class boys were entering the many newly founded public schools, and when increasing attention was given to preparing young men to serve the empire. A new kind of masculinity – and it certainly was not the only one – emerged out of a moment of hybridity where the restrained young gentleman-scholar and man of leisure had to be matched up with the competitive individualistic spirit of the athletic boy. Similarly, the old style of upper-class 'Corinthian' bully had to learn to box, as did the middle classes, fairly and squarely. The late Victorian public schoolboy – the one trained to fit into the most powerful elite in Britain – was the bearer of somewhat incompatible ideologies of gender. He was to be morally respectable, on the one hand, and heroically adventurous, on the other. Put another way, in order to be acceptable to the rules and regulations of his school, he had to keep breaking them.

There is no single or simple reason to explain why the public schools imposed their ban on sexual relations between boys; middle-class religious moralizing would seem to be one, especially in the light of the homosexual scandals that broke during the 1870s and 1880s, and which gave the new sensationalizing press a field-day. Yet the prevention of homo-sexual relations certainly seemed to keep a sense of order among the boys. It is precisely for this reason that homosexuality is banned in the armed services – it is, supposedly, a threat to authority. I do not feel we should turn round on this ban on homosexuality and argue that its threat is purely mythical. Although the ban has been, and still is, used to project and displace fears about male sexuality (its slipping and sliding in and out of homosexuality), the homophobia it generates neces-sarily leads to a more integrated and selective homosociality between men. In these all-male communities, men have to work closely together – but not that closely, lest disobedience and, worse, treachery take place. In this way, the male homosexual – as he became known by 1900 (at least) – would become the ultimate enemy within the nation. With his desires consigned to secrecy, he came to represent secrecy itself in an underworld of coded meanings. By the end of the nineteenth century, the 'closet,' as we now know it only too well, had been assembled, and the writing on the wall has been there ever since. Much more research needs to be done to comprehend how and why it was put there, and the amount of untold violence it has done to the 'homosocial continuum.' In the next section, I want to consider how we might think about classroom practice in (oblique) con-nection with the writing plastered over the lavatory wall.

FROM THE BATHROOM TO THE CLASSROOM

I probably overestimate the changes in consciousness that can and do take place in the very large seminars I facilitate, in great numbers, for most of the academic year. Students are often willing to please, and they no doubt sometimes say things in their essays that are there to win my favor: being a student always requires a good deal of careful planning. It is not uncommon for different tutors to receive entirely different essays from the same student. At the expense of sounding truly patronizing, I am always aware that, given the burden of authority that always hangs over my teaching identity, there is inevitably an awkward mismatch between what I want from my students and what they want from me. On the whole, I think we struggle through. But their plans and my plans are not, cannot, and will not ever be the same. That said, I work on the principle that what we read, and what they write about, are, in some loosely defined way, 'political.' Since I teach English, I am keen to identify how the narratives, plays, and poems we routinely work through bear cultural meanings that speak both to and for us – even if they may seem historically remote. Any seminar carries with it a host of multiple obligations – to say something about form, genre, and language, and something about culture and society, and to articulate these things in a structure where everybody can do something either on their own or in small groups, and feel comfortable with it. Even if the term is a much-distorted one, there is a lot to be said for 'student-centered' learning: to build up confidence, to get students to identify questions for themselves, to make students more interested in devising their own forms of assessment, and to produce a better group dynamic. (In Britain, fortunately, flexible examination systems often provide the opportunity to surmount the 'grades' mania that would appear to afflict so much teaching in US and Canadian colleges.) In the most successful seminars, I have to do very little 'teaching' as such, and, on those occasions, I can step slightly out of role and become a participant. I mention all of this because it is in the classroom where most of my discourse on gender runs back and forth. In my everyday work, as a junior member of staff teaching English, I'm hurriedly rushing from one end of the syllabus to the other in classrooms with 15–20 students with a more or less consistent mix. About two-thirds of the group will be women; about one third will be 'mature' or 'non-traditional' or 'non-standard' students; and most of us will be white. In a British polytechnic, in some respects similar to the American two-year community college, there is a more noticeable proportion of working-class students than you'd be likely to find in a university context here. Among the staff, male teachers are just in the majority (I am the only one who identifies as gay). Feminism – in various forms – is firmly on the syllabus. It is, then, a more equally gendered environment than most to be working in – which is not to suggest it is perfect.

One of the things the department I work in has a commitment to is creative writing – which takes up perhaps a quarter of the students' time in the first two years of a three-year bachelor's degree. The idea, an unusual one in Britain, is to get them writing in forms and styles so that they can better comprehend the literary texts they are analyzing in other parts of the course. They move from learning about handling metrical pause to writing radio documentaries. Many of our students publish their work. They are, therefore, respected as writers as well as readers – although I sometimes wonder whether they are developing a politicized awareness of what it means to take up a genre, use it, and transform it in their own terms. In other words, I am concerned whether they discuss – at a theoretical level – exactly what they feel writing is doing for them as writers.

Perhaps, at this juncture, I may seem to be straying far from the concerns of men and feminism. But let me make one or two more points about writing and reading practice to indicate how gender might be rethought within the syllabus I teach. I do not offer the following suggestions as a cure to the problem of masculinity but to place it, as a problem, within a larger institutional framework. I am a firm believer that historical knowledge, located within what I will call here, provisionally, a self-actualizing structure, can bring about change. By that I mean that once we can see how our lives have been historically produced – even narrated – then we can reach a point of enablement to make positive alterations in our everyday practices of living. In this respect, forms of therapy have their uses, as does the writing of autobiography – although both have been condemned for their bourgeois individualism. I'm not interested in divagating into the polemics of individualism and its discontents at this stage of the argument; what does concern me here is how I can create a structure in my teaching where students have the opportunity to understand how their identities – their multiple identities – have been shaped by historical forces.

One way of opening up this discussion in the classroom is to embark on a writing exercise where we decide to tell, not our own stories, but the stories of our parents or carers when they were the same age as we are now. Once we have got a short piece of text together, we can then split into small groups to discuss various things: the choices that shaped the life in question; and the narrative devices used to shape the account of that life. In other words, we are beginning to consider how we construct a life story for ourselves. At a later stage, we can move on to the practice of autobiography, and thereby consider how we can make sense of our stories as pieces of history. This is a complex topic but it is one I'm concerned with because it seems to me that learning to write about self-identity can – I don't say will – offer the chance to change that self. For men – particularly men brought up to believe never to question their subjectivities – this can be extremely productive. Speaking of, and writing about, the self (a far from stable thing), even in a supportive atmosphere, can be stressful (as can any learning experience). But within a formal framework – where the discussion is around point of view, choice of language, genre – it is possible to avoid making people feel guilty or inadequate about the life stories they are writing. The important thing to do is to get them thinking about how they are constituted by their own stories. As students gather confidence around this use of life writing, they may, perhaps, glimpse the chance to change the script.

In the context of research into life writing, the now sizable body of work by the labour historian and educationist, Carolyn Steedman, is crucial. One of her books, *The Radical Soldier's Tale* (1988), shows how a member of the uniformed working class, John Pearman, discovered, during the course of writing his memoirs, how he was historically situated: how, in other words, he had come to account for himself, as a man, in this way.[10] In her analysis of Pearman's memoir, Steedman makes frequent reference to the writings of Raymond Williams, notably Williams' often nebulous formulation of 'structure of feeling' whereby emotional response to the world works together with a cognitive understanding of that world.[11] Life writing provides one possibility – one needed urgently, I think, by men – to find a structure of feeling where they can think and feel, simultaneously, about how and why they have been placed within the patriarchal order of things, and how, in their own ways, they might shift that order. I suppose I am making a plea for a 'long revolution' for men (which I have tried to suggest began, confusedly, with Millett's *Sexual Politics*). At this point, I can turn to some examples of a visibly new (but not entirely positive) male discourse. It is still hard to know what to call these 'new men' who are trying, as best they can, to tell us about how they want to change as men. Should they be called, in this labelling exercise, anti-masculinist and/or anti-sexist? Or just plain radical? As we shall see, this apparent radicalism among straight-identified men is still in its narcissistic infancy.

RADICAL MALE DISCOURSE?

Men (straight-identified men) have, indeed, begun – slowly but surely – to write about their own place within the academy, and their (uneasy) relationship with feminism. I won't go over the rather prolix debates that preoccupy Alice Jardine and Paul Smith's jointly edited collection of essays, rather offensively entitled *Men in Feminism* (1987) – where a number of contributors ponder the thrusting movement of this text.[12] Nor will I move into the rather sterile question of 'male feminism' (where men may feel they need feminism but feminism knows it does not need men). Most of the essays included in *Men in Feminism* are hampered by the fact that they produce an introspective discourse, where one essay accretes around another – a symptom of the Modern Language Association panel format from which much of the contents sprang. That said, this collection does attempt to get some discussion moving in a conversational form. The tone is frequently personal, if not confessional. But for all the sensitivity and openness the (straight) male contributors show towards their feminist interlocutors, little care or respect is demonstrated towards lesbian and gay politics. No lesbian response to 'male feminism' is to be seen in these pages, and only one gay male voice can be heard at the margins of the debate. Its consideration of maleness is almost exclusively about male heterosexuality.

Another book which attempts to mobilize its contents in a dialogic manner, so that some sense of debate is going on between the papers, is Linda Kauffman's *Gender and Theory* (1989), where radical men present themselves as rarely before: emotionally on display. Just a second ago, I raised the possibility of using autobiography for changing (straight-identified) male subjectivity. After all, straight men are, in academic work, so infrequently asked to question the powerful sense of agency that loads the prefigurative and patriarchal energy of their sentences. So, here, in *Gender and Theory*, it is particularly interesting to see a man speak of himself as a man speaking of himself (the pleonasm is unavoidable). The example I want to look at comes from an essay by Gerald M. MacClean – which, like my own, discusses reading, critical practice, and pedagogy. I will quote a long extract from it that points up a number of problematic features in the 'self-actualizing' of the radical male voice. (Importantly,

MacClean is trying to take up some of the suggestions made by Jardine in *Men in Feminism* about how men must learn to 'speak of their bodies.')[13] MacClean has this singularly distressing tale to tell:

I was teaching in Ontario, my first post-doctoral appointment. Donna [Landry; MacClean's partner] and I had begun our first year of professional separation in September: how could she turn down the offer of a job at Princeton? I had just arrived back in Kingston from driving her to Syracuse airport when an uncle in Toronto phoned with the news of [my] Mother's death.

Two years later I told all this to a psychiatrist in Ann Arbor as the occasion for my being there to see him. I had just read Alice Miller's book about 'gifted' children and felt what all readers are encouraged to feel, that I hadn't grieved properly. The previous year Donna had resigned from Princeton for a terminal appointment at Michigan that coincided with my move to Detroit. That winter, during a period of gloom which reading Miller led me to associate with guilt over Mother's death, I had hit Donna during an argument over nothing that important. This must not happen again. The analyst wanted a contract of two hours a week for a minimum of four years. As part of commitment to analysis, I was to pay for all sessions, even those I knew I couldn't attend. He told me I had un-resolved problems with my mother, which was of course no more than I had told him on arrival. I didn't sign up. I couldn't afford the percentage my insurance wouldn't pay. And after the diagnostic sessions I no longer felt that problems with Mother had very much to do with the specific problem of my violence. I was already aware of an important body of work being done on male violence, but began to notice how this knowledge is typically constituted as a science of the other. When I learned just how common 'domestic' violence is, I recall being both horrified and amazed since my own experi-ence had seemed so unusual. While living the contradiction that what I did may be 'normal' but not therefore legitimate (or even very much like the paradigms offered), I remain convinced that institutional privileges and pressures, a whole lifetime of them yet to be encountered, still bear more directly than my 'earliest affective experience with [my] mother.' I am surprised still, when talking about this, to find how many men and women have personal experience of violence. The knowledge that my act was really not so unusual is no comfort. Rather it has made me angry at the way we all put up with so much that is intolerable. In terms of scholarship, for example, there is the way historians continue to ignore the struggles and achievements of women, the problem at which I began directing my research.[14]

I take MacClean's writing as an instance of a would-be gender-politicized man trying to find words to face up to an appalling act about which he still feels guilty. The posture he takes up is, for a male academic, a rather unexpected one. But there is something incredibly naive (or, possibly, disingenuous) about it. He seems to have come across the fact of violence – as the doer of the deed (not, we notice, as victim) – as a complete innocent. He also seems anxious to displace his guilt onto his grief, so that the act of violence is represented as a symptom of his sense of loss (his mother's death). (Damage to one woman has been produced by the loss of another. That is the unpleasant equation worked out, but not analyzed, here.) Moreover, professional life appears to have to bear the blame and burden of the sins of the fathers in this appalling (if routine) incident. That violence – of the type we see written up in men's bathrooms – might be a constituent of male identity (rather than of the ungendered 'gifted' child) is a thought that eludes him. Proffered as an 'honest' piece of self-disclosure, with some sort of awareness of the politics of gender ('the struggles and achievements of women'), it nonetheless stands as an evasive kind of confession. The reader, it may well be thought, is supposed to act here as a substitute for the analyst; but I think we might impose a much more severe contract on MacClean – and turn this discourse back on itself to ask whether he can examine his conscience and find himself wanting in ways he is, at present, somewhat unwilling to admit.

There is always something irritating about straight men – the ones with greater entitlements than most – opening up their psychical wounds as a cover for the damage they have been permitted to do in the violent practices of everyday life. It need not cheer us that one among their company has found reason to declare his wrongs, as if the collection of essays in which he appears is some kind of tribunal – and that we are there to act as arbiters upon his wealth of bad feeling. It is, surely, possible to 'come out' as a straight man, one wishing to change, without resorting to confession of this kind. At times, 'coming out,' outside its lesbian and gay context, is confused with the structure of confession. To 'come out,' to claim a sexual-political identity, is not, for lesbians and gay men, to reveal some shameful fact of one's being but to partake in a community of interests. Sadly, this confessional style is becoming altogether too commonplace. A recent British example of the soul-baring mode can be found in Victor Seidler's *Rediscovering Masculinity* (1989), where the author tells a far from celebratory story of how he, as a former hard-line Trotskyist, became disillusioned with standing outside factory gates selling radical newspapers, and so discovered himself via 'Red Therapy.'[15] Seidler's is a book full of guilt, all couched in a self-indulgent tone that would seem to replicate the very forms of egotism on which a more conventional masculinity is, we might imagine, predicated. So of what can radical straight-identified men speak? They might, for a start, consider how the 'homosocial continuum' locates them within a phobic space (like a bathroom cubicle) with misogynistic pictures of women on one side set against homophobic accusations on the other. They could then consider how and why this horrendous construction has placed them (whether they like it or not) precisely there, and how they might elect to change it. There are some kinds of autobiography that may well assist this transformation – bringing the straight male life-writer to a point of enablement to see how his gendered script has been written. It is time for straight men to do what Kate Millett started more than twenty years ago: to supply theoretically attentive and historically informed readings of Mailer, Miller, Lawrence, and many, many more, and not disavow their relations (possibly similarities) to these male texts. They may care to read Genet and other gay male writers alongside them as interpretive devices to expose how male heterosexuality maintains its power base. (MacClean, for instance, engages with feminism but not gay critique. I am sure that so-called 'male feminists' – of the kind to be found in *Men in Feminism* – are unlikely, at the moment, to identify, in any way, as gay. Gayness is, all too clearly, a completely 'other' zone, an implicit irrelevancy.)

In decades to come, straight-identified men may have something as revolutionary as (and workable with) feminist and anti-homophobic critique for when it comes to 'speaking of gender.' By that point, perhaps, the phobic boundaries marked out along the 'homosocial' network on man-to-man relations will have been changed to the degree that we are no longer identified as gay or straight, feminist or (anti)masculinist, but are in possession of altogether unforeseen identities. It may well be that the 'homosocial continuum' will become, not subordinately, but predominantly, a 'homosexual' one – with all men discovering their ability to love, not fear, one another. I, for one, would like to think MacClean might be my ally, but we need to discuss the forms of gendered discourse through which we might begin to hear one another. Yet the words we have at present are not adequate to the sexualities we might care to develop. Luce Irigaray's concept of 'hom(m)osexuality' is a by now notorious example of how the theorization of man-to-man relations can become blocked at the political level.[16] Irigaray's awkward, unhelpful punning on the 'hom(m)osexual' structure that supposedly binds men together collapses the taboo on male same-sex desire with the workings of patriarchy – a patriarchy which clearly benefits straight-identified men. This is precisely the error that Millett made more than twenty years ago. I close with Irigaray's provocative (and damaging) pun because her influential work provides some indication of how far the sexual-political analysis of masculinity – whether in the bathroom or the classroom – has yet to go.

NOTES

My thanks to David Porter for his scrupulous editing and for inviting me to give an early version of this paper in the 'Men and Feminism' series of seminars organized at St John's College, Cambridge in the spring of 1990, and to members of the Critical Theory seminar at the University of Nottingham for sustained (if, at times, unsupportive) discussion of the issues at stake. This paper was completed while I was working in the School of Cultural Studies at Sheffield City Polytechnic.

1   Cora Kaplan, 'Radical Feminism and Literature: Rethinking Millett's *Sexual Politics*' in *Sea Changes: Culture and Feminism* (London: Verso, 1986), 15–30. It is not my intention to anatomize Millett's study; references are to the Virago edition (London, 1977).

2   Kaplan, *Sea Changes*, 25. Compare Toril Moi's unforgiving critique of Millett's amnesia towards earlier feminist theorists: '[The] astonishing absence in a feminist writer of due recognition of her feminist precursors is also evident in Millett's treatment of women authors. We have already seen that she dismisses Virginia Woolf in one brief passage; in fact,

with the sole exception of Charlotte Bronte, *Sexual Politics* deals exclusively with male authors. It is as if Millett wishes consciously or unconsciously to suppress the evidence of earlier patriarchal works, not least if her precursors were women' (*Sexual/Textual Politics: Feminist Literary Theory* (London: Methuen, 1985), 25).

3   Juliet Mitchell corrects Millett's errors in 'Kate Millett: Freud, Facts and Fantasies' in *Psychoanalysis and Feminism* (Harmondsworth: Pelican Books, 1974), 351–55. Mitchell is referring to Millett, *Sexual Politics*, 176–89. Mitchell's work, in its gradual movement away from the materialism of the British New Left of the 1950s and 1960s, has been sharply criticized by Julia Swindells and Lisa Jardine in their *What's Left? Women in Culture and the Labour Movement* (London: Routledge, 1990), 69–93. The difference between Mitchell's and Swindells and Jardine's respective positions points up one of several fundamental splits within British feminism.

4   I could cite several examples of feminist homophobia. One recent instance will indicate the difficulties that can lie in the way of feminist–antihomophobic alliances: 'I distrust male homosexuals because they choose men over women just as our social and political institutions, but they too share in the struggle against bipolar gender constraints, against the compulsory choice of masculine or feminine' (Jane Gallop, *Thinking through the Body* (New York: Columbia University Press, 1989), 113). Choosing men 'over women'? Here, in this muddled but nonetheless telling formulation, male same-sex desire would seem caught in a double bind between choosing to challenge the sex/gender hierarchy and in so doing derogating women.

5   Eve Kosofsky Sedgwick, *Between Men: English Literature and Male Homosocial Desire* (New York: Columbia University Press, 1985). Among the many recent books deeply influenced by Sedgwick's work is Richard Dellamora, *Masculine Desire: The Sexual Politics of Victorian Aestheticism* (Chapel Hill: University of North Carolina Press, 1990).

6   Rich's concept of a 'lesbian continuum' appears in 'Compulsory Heterosexuality and Lesbian Existence,' *Signs: Journal of Women in Culture and Society*, 5:4 (1980), 631–660, and is reprinted in Ann Snitow, Christine Stansell, and Sharon Thompson, eds., *Desire: The Politics of Sexuality* (London: Virago Press, 1984). In this exceptionally valuable analysis of women's oppression, Rich, too, would seem to have a selective view of male homosexuality: 'Part of the history of lesbian existence is, obviously, to be found where lesbians, lacking a coherent female community, have shared a kind of social life and common cause with homosexual men. But this has to be seen against the differences: women's lack of economic and cultural privilege relative to men; qualitative differences in female and male relationships, for example, the prevalence of anonymous sex and the justification of pederasty among male homosexuals, the pronounced ageism of male homosexual standards of sexual attractiveness' (228).

7   Gayle Rubin, 'The Traffic in Women: Notes on the "Political Economy of Sex"' in Rayna R. Reiter, ed., *Toward an Anthropology of*

Women (New York: Monthly Review Press, 1975). For a scrupulous reading of the limits to Rubin's critique of Lévi-Strauss, see Judith Butler, *Gender Trouble: Feminism and the Subversion of Identity* (London: Routledge, 1990), 72–77.

8   The homophobia/misogyny boundary circumscribes the dispiriting exchange between David van Leer and Sedgwick in the pages of *Critical Inquiry*. The debate revolves around Sedgwick's exceptionally powerful essay, 'The Beast in the Closet: James and the Writing of Homosexual Panic' in Ruth Bernard Yeazell, ed., *Sex, Politics, and Science in the Nineteenth-Century Novel*, Selected Papers from the English Institute, No.10 (Baltimore: The Johns Hopkins University Press, 1986), 147–86, reprinted in Elaine Showalter, ed., *Speaking of Gender* (New York: Routledge, 1989), 243–68, and revised and reprinted in *Epistemology of the Closet* (Hemel Hempstead: Harvester-Wheatsheaf Press, 1990). See Van Leer, 'The Beast of the Closet: Homosociality and the Pathology of Manhood,' *Critical Inquiry* 15 (1989), 587–605; Sedgwick, 'Critical Response I: Tide and Trust,' *Critical Inquiry* 15 (1989), 745–57; and Van Leer, 'Critical Response II: Trust and Trade,' *Critical Inquiry* 15 (1989), 758–63. The marginalization of lesbian desire in Sedgwick's *Between Men* is examined in Terry Castle, 'Sylvia Townsend Warner and the Counter-plot of Lesbian Fiction,' *Textual Practice* 4:2 (1990), 213–35 reprinted in Joseph Bristow, ed., *Sexual Sameness: Textual Differences in Lesbian and Gay Writing* (London: Routledge, 1992).

9   Joseph Bristow, *Empire Boys: Adventures in a Man's World* (London: Harper Collins Academic, 1991).

10   Carolyn Steedman, *The Radical Soldier's Tale: John Pearman, 1819–1908* (London: Routledge, 1988). I have developed some of the issues raised here about the usefulness of Williams' idea of 'structure of feeling' in 'Life Stories: Carolyn Steedman's History Writing,' *New Formations* 13 (1991), 113–31.

11   On 'structure of feeling,' see Williams, *Marxism and Literature* (London: Oxford University Press, 1977), 132.

12   Alice Jardine and Paul Smith, eds., *Men in Feminism* (New York: Methuen, 1987).

13   Gerald M. MacClean, 'Citing the Subject' in Linda Kauffman, ed., *Gender and Theory: Dialogues on Feminist Criticism* (Oxford: Basil Blackwell, 1989), 153. MacClean is referring to Alice Jardine, 'Men in Feminism: Odor di Uomo Or Compagnons de Route' in Alice Jardine and Paul Smith, eds., *Men In Feminism*, 61. MacClean is not citing directly from Jardine, who says: 'In the deeper realms of psycho-analytic inquiry, . . . you [men – all men? straight-identified men? 'male feminists'?] have not even begun to think about your mothers. Nor have you rewritten your relationship with your fathers. For example, how would a male critic after feminism rewrite Harold Bloom's *Anxiety of Influence* ([New York: Oxford University Press, 1973])? What else? Well, there's men's relationship *after feminism*, to death, scopophilia, fetishism (we've had a beginning today), the penis and balls, erection, ejaculation (not to mention the phallus),

paranoia, homosexuality [the 'other' here], blood, tactile pleasure, pleasure in general, *desire* . . . '. MacClean has obviously tried to fulfil these prescriptions. To get straight-identified men back to their estranged bodies, perhaps Jardine could recommend a few gay classics (such as Genet's) to the 'men' of whom she is speaking, and maybe MacClean could start thinking about them?

Jardine's and MacClean's conjoint discourse is simply symptomatic of the exclusion through non-acknowledgement of gay men within an emerging 'men's studies' or 'male feminism.' I take the point, made by some members of the Nottingham seminar, that MacClean is offering himself up here as a 'soft target,' and that my 'ungenerous' reading of his text may have the effect of 'silencing' straight-identified men attempting to articulate a sexual politics of their own. The dialog, however, has to start somewhere. Altogether more wide-ranging than *Men in Feminism* in terms of the male subject-positions it explores – even if the whole book is exclusively focused within literary studies – is Joseph A. Boone and Michael Cadden (eds) *Engendering Men: The Question of Male Feminist Criticism* (New York: Routledge, 1990). On the achievements of *Engendering Men*, see my 'Male Wants,' *Paragraph* 14 (1991), 297–305.

14 MacClean, 'Citing the Subject,' 151–52. In this passage, he footnotes Alice Miller, *The Drama of the Gifted Child*, translated by Ruth Ward (New York: Basic Books, 1981) and refers to several recent studies involved in the 'recovery of the lives, works and achievements of early English feminists' (155). A great many other points could be raised about this objectionable piece of writing. I will make one further observation: MacClean's reference to his mother's death closely resembles Stephen Heath's meditation on his 'admiration' for feminism where Heath recalls writing his essay at his dying mother's bedside: 'Male Feminism' in *Men in Feminism*, 30.

15 Victor J. Seidler, *Rediscovering Masculinity: Reason, Language and Sexuality* (London: Routledge, 1989). Since I completed the present essay, two books which lay a stress on male life-writing practice have been published. Both are much more successful in their methods than Seidler's: David Cohen, *Being a Man* (London: Routledge, 1990), and David Jackson, *Unmasking Masculinity: A Critical Autobiography* (London: Unwin Hyman, 1990).

16 Luce Irigaray, *This Sex Which Is Not One*, trans. Catherine Porter with Carolyn Burke (Ithaca: Cornell University Press, 1985), 172. As Diana Fuss says, in Irigaray's formulation 'real homosexual men drop out of the analysis': *Essentially Speaking: Feminism, Nature and Difference* (New York: Routledge, 1990), 49. Fuss's exemplary analysis of the essentialism–constructionism double bind is especially sensitive to the exclusion and/or distortion of gay male sexuality in feminist and non-feminist writings on sex and gender. (Incidentally, 'hom(m)o-sexual' could be read as a piece of anti-lesbian sloganizing, with its 'mannish' connotations.) Some might argue that Irigaray's frequently cited-out-of-context term has become a scapegoat for all sorts of uncertainties within sexual-political discourse.

Chapter 5

Body odor
Gay male semiotics and *l'écriture féminine*

Gregory W. Bredbeck

> And sometimes when your eloquence escapes you
> Their logic ties you up and rapes you
> (The Police, from the album *Cenyatta Mondatta*, 1980)

The body seduces us, not just sexually, but also politically. Its (supposed) tangibility, its (supposed) materiality, and its (supposed) testimony to experience empower and enforce almost every subaltern insurrection, as well as most hegemonic ideologies. Plato's Aristophanes, seeking to account for the diversity of sexual behavior in humans, posited a hermaphroditic, undifferentiated *ur*-body from which the male and female bodies are separated (59–62). Thomas Hobbes, 'rationally' anatomizing the components of a commonwealth in 1651, traced power through the 'inevitability' of the flesh: 'Reward and Punishment . . . are the nerves, that do the same in the Body Naturall' (81). The populist American feminists of the 1970s, seeking to empower the 'common' woman, championed the amateur medical text *Our Bodies, Ourselves*. Gay liberationists opposing anti-sodomy legislation and pro-choice lobbyists advocating the right to abortion currently carry a common banner: 'Keep your laws off our bodies.' I, like these various positions, fetishize the body. And yet what is a fetish? An impossibility – the *phallic mother*, an oxymoron, the always already absent object of desire.

The very title, *Our Bodies, Ourselves*, begins to suggest the sort of problematic we encounter when we write of/from the body. The 'self,' we know, is by and large a no-thing, a false unity or chimera. What does it mean, then, that politically it can be chiasmically intervalidated with the body, locked into the feminist algebraic, body = self? An equation is bi-directional, and thus while adding the 'tangibility' of the 'body' to the self, it also (and more accurately) attributes the vacuousness of the 'self' to the body. In order to achieve the material assertion of the body demanded by the statement, this latter possibility must necessarily, and erroneously, be suppressed. And yet no matter how problematical, the very centrality of the body within Western ontology also makes it a potent guarantor of authority, a viable site of resistance – an *essential* political tool.

The problematic with which I am dealing here has a long and varied history, and has generally been forced to a certain crisis around the Cartesian binarism of mind/body. The binarism opens two possibilities: I think, therefore I am; I am, therefore I think. The suppression of this duality has long been the stake of the philosophical theorization of the body. To paraphrase Jane Gallop, the history of Western philosophy's inscribing of the mind/body dichotomy has been a constant attempt to render the body subordinate to man-made meaning.[1] What we speak of when we speak of the body, then, is not the *thing* itself, but its status as a site of ontological authority. By extension, the control of the body *as* authority becomes a condition for speech itself. It is no coincidence, as numerous scholars have pointed out, that hysteria is figured as a radical rupture between body and self, nor that it has been vectored toward certain specific bodies: the female body, the homosexual male body, and so forth.

My ability to sketch this introductory problematic is, of course, the result of the pioneering and now largely discredited work of post-1968 French feminism, especially that of Luce Irigaray and Hélène Cixous, amalgamated by American feminism under the neologisms *l'écriture féminine* and *parler femme*. *L'écriture féminine* has been vilified as obscurantist, elitist, homogenizing and, above all, essentialist. I do not intend to mount a defense of the *école* against these charges. Rather, my purpose here will be to read *l'écriture féminine* otherwise, to see which of its facets and strategies might lend direction to a gay male semiotic practice. Ultimately I will suggest that the perceived shortcomings of *l'écriture féminine* do not result from its reliance on the body, but from its reliance on a body that is specifically but subtly coded as heterosexual. Gay male theory, along with its closely related allies, lesbian theory and queer theory, is at a point now where ways of asserting the authority of the body can be deduced without also reinscribing the body as heterosexual. However, the outcome of this practice, I will claim, results in a body that frustrates the tenets of atemporality and materiality that have typically been the ideological conditions of the body.

THE HETEROSEXUAL BODY

> Woman 'touches herself' all the time, and moreover no one can forbid her to do so, for her genitals are formed of two lips in continuous contact. Thus, within herself, she is already two – but not divisible into one(s) – that caress each other.
>
> (*This Sex* 24)

Irigaray's famous appeal to a labial authority – to the psycho-biological conditions that allow women's 'lips to speak together' (205–218) – is at once the most obvious and obfuscating appearance of the body in French feminism. Its direct and specific assertion of the female body echoes the broader tropes of other theorists. Cixous, for example, in her manifesto 'The Laugh of the Medusa,' calls for a return to woman's 'immense bodily territories which have been kept under seal' (250). And Marguerite Duras has mandated that 'We must move on to the rhetoric of women, one that is anchored in the organism, in the body' (Husserl-Kapit 434).

The American response to the French feminist body has been less than totally accepting. Ann Rosalind Jones, in her germinal review essays of French feminism, summarizes the problem perceived in *l'écriture féminine*:

> All in all, at this point in history, most of us perceive our bodies through a jumpy, contradictory mesh of hoary sexual symbolization and political counter-response. It is possible to argue that the French feminists make of the female body too unproblematically pleasurable and totalized an entity.
>
> ('Writing the Body' 93)[2]

And yet the 'unproblematical' body in *l'écriture féminine* is also overtly problematized, for it is not necessarily the thing itself. Cixous prefaces her 'body' with the disclaimer that 'you can't talk about *a* female sexuality, uniform, homogeneous, classifiable into codes' ('Laugh' 246). Her topic is 'a universal woman subject who must bring women to their senses and to their meaning in history' (245). The oppositional structure of this latter sentence is telling.

'Universal woman' is contradistinct to 'women in history.' The homogenizing woman who underpins the polemic is isolated as a construct meant to affect, but not simply to be, the materiality of women. Cixous's process can be clarified through Irigaray's own defense: 'To play with mimesis is thus, for a woman, to try to recognize the place of her exploitation by discourse, without allowing herself to be simply reduced to it' (*This Sex* 76). Diana Fuss, in her wide-reaching reassessment of essentialism in contemporary feminist practice, has argued that the theorization of Irigaray is not essentialist, but *strategically* essential – that it deploys an essentialized body in a calculated manner designed to disrupt other sites of authority (55–72). Fuss's argument is part of a broader current project designed to rethink the notion of essence and to break the paranoid grip that anti-essentialism has on feminist theory; and as my presentation indicates, I agree with such a project.[3] However, the point that interests my argument is not *what* the body means in *l'écriture féminine*, but rather *how* it means. For the theorizations of both Cixous and Irigaray construct systems of representation based on the 'body' that mimetically reinscribe certain semiotic hierarchies that, I will claim, replicate and maintain heterosexuality.

To begin, it is *essential* to recognize that sexuality is not a descriptive discourse, but a constitutive one. Irigaray herself says as much in *Speculum of the Other Woman*. Illuminating the 'blind spots' in Freud's essay, 'Femininity,' she demonstrates that

> In fact, science 'tells you something that runs counter to your expectations and is probably calculated to confuse your [and its?] feelings. It draws your attention to the fact that portions of the male sexual apparatus also appear in women's bodies, though in atrophied state and vice versa in the alternative case' (p. 114). Science thus forces you to see in the objective fact 'the indications of *bisexuality* [Freud's italics], as though an individual is not a man or a woman but always both' (p. 114). You are then man and woman. Man, or woman? Yet – you may be assured, reassured – one character always prevails over the other.
>
> (*Speculum* 14)

The assumption behind such formulations, Irigaray claims, is 'that the psychic is prescribed by the anatomical according to a *mimetic order*, with anatomical science imposing the truth of its model upon "psychological behaviour." In intercourse, man and woman *mime* the type of relationship between sperm and ovum' (15). Anatomy is destiny. Gender relations become inevitable because they are 'naturally' associated with the biology that gives rise to them. And yet, as Irigaray's reading of Freud shows, the biology giving rise to gender roles is always already constructed by a gendered representation. And hence the 'body' in 'science' is inevitably anatomized across the gendered axis it supposedly originates: it is always man, always woman, or always both. The 'objective' gaze that can find a disruptive bisexuality preceding man and woman (but really just woman) also always finds sexuality – 'bi' or not – where it looks. It is not the body that determines gender, but gender that determines the body; by which I mean, the system of representation labeled as 'gender' in Western cultures posits the already gendered body as its deferred origin and authority. It is with this formula in mind that Teresa de Lauretis has offered her influential theorization of 'the technology of gender,' of which I offer here only part:

> (1) Gender is (a) representation – which is not to say that it does not have concrete or real implications, both social and subjective, for the material life of individuals. On the contrary,
> (2) The representation of gender *is* its construction – and in the simplest sense it can be said that all of Western art and high culture is the engraving of that construction . . . .
>
> (*Technologies* 3)

'Gender,' de Lauretis summarizes, 'is not only the effect of representation but also its excess, what remains outside discourse as a potential trauma which can rupture or destabilize, if not contained, any representation' (3).

The second *essential* point in my argument is that gender difference and sexual difference are not the same – though they are frequently expressed through each other. As first set forth by Gayle Rubin, 'Gender affects the operation of the sexual system, and the sexual system has had gender-specific manifestations. But although sex and gender are related, they are not the same thing' (307). The distinction Rubin makes can be demonstrated through the heterosexually imposed stereotypes of the 'feminine faggot' and the 'masculine dyke.' In both cases movements away from orthodox positions on the axis of sexual difference are expressed through a movement on the axis of gender difference; a 'broach' of bedroom etiquette is articulated through a slippage of gender identity. Rubin's formulation enables us to separate and analyze two primary binarisms that are posited as chiasmically dependent within Western ontology: man/woman and homosexual/heterosexual.[4] The distinction between these separate axes is of central importance, for it allows us to see how the liberational *gender* representations of *l'écriture féminine* can, simultaneously, create *sexually* conservative hierarchies.

And what are these hierarchies I keep speaking of? They are *representational* assumptions, strategies of form, not content. Indeed, both Cixous and Irigaray use sexual differences such as lesbianism, (male) homosexuality and bisexuality as topics in the content of their theories. Lesbianism and bisexuality become anti-dotes to misogyny for Cixous. 'The Americans remind us, "We are all Lesbians",' which is interpreted as meaning, 'don't denigrate woman, don't make her what men have made you' ('Laugh' 252). Of bisexuality we are told:

> In saying 'bisexual, hence neuter,' I am referring to the classic conception of bisexuality, which, squashed under the emblem of castration fear and along with the fantasy of a 'total' being (though composed of two halves), would do away with the difference experienced as an operation incurring loss, as the mark of dreaded sectility.
>
> (254)

To which Cixous opposes

> . . . the *other bisexuality* on which every subject not enclosed in the false theater of phallocentric representationalism has founded his/her erotic universe. Bisexuality: that is, each one's location in self (*réperage en soi*) of the presence – variously manifest and insistent according to each person, male or female – of both sexes, non-exclusion either of the difference or of one sex, and, from this 'self-permission,' multiplication of the effect of the inscription of desire, over all parts of my body and the other body.
>
> (254)[5]

Irigaray, in the influential essays 'Women on the Market' and 'Commodities among Themselves,' claims that 'the possibility of our social life, of our culture, depends upon a ho(m)mo-sexual monopoly' (*This Sex* 171), and asks

Why is masculine homosexuality considered exceptional, then, when in fact the economy as a whole is based upon it? Why are homosexuals ostracized, when society postulates homosexuality?

(192)[6]

Sexual differences in these instances are part of a multiplicitous thematic, a content that recognizes a diversity contradictory to the reductionism of traditional (hetero)sexual formulations.

This plural content is, however – to borrow Cixous's apt words – 'squashed under' a less pluralistic mimetic strategy. For to discern the place of the body in these theorizations is also to discover the 'place' of deferral that empowers heterosexual representation. Critiquing Lacan's *Encore, Le Seminaire XX*, Irigaray tells us that 'a woman' is 'a body-matter marked by their [men's] signifiers, a prop for their souls-fantasies' (*This Sex* 96). Woman reminds us that 'sexual pleasure is engulfed then in the body of the Other. It is "produced" because the Other, in part, escapes the grasp of discourse' (97). Disentangling the ideological assumptions of fluid mechanics, she claims that 'all [theories] have excluded from their mode of symbolization *certain properties of real fluids*,' and further states that 'certainly these "theoretical" fluids have enabled the technical – also mathematical – form of analysis to progress, while losing a certain relationship to *the reality of bodies in the process*' (109). Exploring the ramifications of hysteria for both men and women, she tells us

Furthermore, I think men would have a lot to gain by being somewhat less repressive about hysteria. For in fact by repressing and censuring hysteria they have secured increased force, or more precisely, increased power, but they have lost a great deal of their relation to their own bodies.

(139)

Irigaray states that her goal is to create a hermeneutic that 'would reject all closure or circularity in discourse – any constitution of *arche* or *telos*' (153) – but her representational strategy speaks otherwise. For in each of these instances there is always something 'other' to discourse, something deferred, removed, and posited as originary to discourse itself. 'Body-matter' precedes 'marks'; Others 'escape' discourse, exist anterior to it; 'real fluids' precede their 'theoretical' counterparts; men's 'own bodies' precede the body as predicated by the censuring of hysteria. There is a distinction here between the physical and the meta-physical, between discourse and its referent – and this distinction is also always vectored so as to designate representation as secondary or after-the-fact. And thus the 'real' always rests inertly beneath imaginary machinations, a 'woman' passively receiving the inscription of (male) metaphysics.

The mimesis I am tracing in Irigaray's discourse can be clari-fied through her own analysis of Plato's mimesis. As she tells us,

> In Plato, there are two *mimeses*. To simplify: there is *mimesis* as production, which would lie more in the realm of music, and there is the *mimesis* that would be already caught up in a process of *imitation, specularization, adequation,* and *reproduc-tion*. It is the second form that is privileged throughout the history of philosophy and whose effects/symptoms, such as latency, suffering, paralysis of desire, are encountered in hysteria. The first form seems always to have been repressed, if only because it was constituted as an enclave within a 'dominant' discourse. Yet it is doubtless in the direction of, and on the basis of, that first *mimesis* that the possibility of a woman's writing may come about.
>
> (131)

Irigaray's distinction again calls into question the difference be-tween constitutive and expressive representation. Constitutive mimesis, which Plato associates with music, stands contradistinct to expressive arts such as painting and poetry, in which the medium supposedly 'channels' a reality which precedes it. The difference between these two modes is also always a *différance*, a repression of the status of *all* representation as constructive of both its subject and object. And yet despite Irigaray's desire for the initial, constitutive mode of mimesis, her structure of deferred referral always invokes the latter, for it presupposes that repre-sentation must be preceded by something real, tangible, true. Traces of this specular mimesis also show forth in Cixous's theorization. 'Write!' she commands woman. 'Writing is for you, you are for you; your body is yours, take it' (246). She continues:

> By writing herself, woman will return to the body which has been more than confiscated from her, which has been turned into the uncanny stranger on display – the ailing or dead

figure, which so often turns out to be the nasty companion, the cause and location of inhibitions. Censor the body and you censor breath and speech at the same time.

(250)

The sentiments here are laudable, but their directionality is reversed – specularized. For to move from expressive to constitutive mimesis we would have to rewrite them: 'for your body to be yours, *make* it'; 'censor the breath and speech and you censor the body at the same time.'

It is worth stressing this mimetic regress in *l'écriture féminine*, for it is, I claim, precisely this reliance on deferral and delay – on, if I can be allowed the reach, reality – that is the representational scene of heterosexuality. To examine this idea, we must turn to another French theorist, Guy Hocquenghem, and his seldom discussed radical gay tract, *Homosexual Desire*. Opening the anus for (among other things) discussion, Hocquenghem traces how specular mimesis – representation as a system of deferral and delay – is the scene through which heterosexuality expresses itself and, *simultaneously*, the scene that represents heterosexuality.

Ours is a phallocratic society, inasmuch as social relationships as a whole are constructed according to a hierarchy which reveals the transcendence of the great signifier. The schoolmaster, the general and the departmental manager are the father-phallus; everything is organised according to the pyramidal mode, by which the Oedipal signifier allocates the various levels and identifications. The body gathers round the phallus like society round the chief. Both those in whom it is absent and those who obey it belong to the kingdom of the phallus: this is the triumph of Oedipus.

(82)

The body here is implicated in the scene of representation. 'It gathers round' the signifier-phallus, and its motility betrays the binarism of body/representation, of referent/reference, that underpins specular mimesis. If we can explain Irigaray's mimesis through Plato, we can explain Hocquenghem's through Nietzsche, who in *The Will to Power* claims that

The fragment of the outside world of which we become conscious comes after the effect that has been produced on us and

is projected *a posteriori* as its 'cause.' In the phenomenalism of
the 'inner world' we invert the chronology of cause and effect.
The basic fact of 'inner experience' is that the cause gets
imagined after the effect has occurred.

(3: 804)

Effect gives rise to cause, representation gives rise to the object
represented.[7] This too is the point that Hocquenghem makes:
phallic, heterosexual representation constructs a cause for its effect,
and it then becomes the task of the phallus to reverse this
temporality and posit the representation of the cause as *a posteriori*.
The object represented is the alibi of representation, the excuse
under which it escapes culpability. If we were to read Oscar Wilde
with the same seriousness we afford Matthew Arnold (although to
do so would be a great disservice to Wilde), we would already know
this: 'Art never expresses anything but itself' (991).

What I am suggesting, then, is a correspondence between the
hierarchicalization of object and expression in mimetic theory
and the hierarchicalization of sexual meanings in phallic heterosexual ontology. For to put Hocquenghem's theorization into its
simplest terms, what phallic heterosexuality does is to posit the
phallic signifier and then inscribe all sexualities as objects/
referents which either find representation in its terms, and
thereby are good, or find no representation, and thereby are bad.
This is also, I think, similar to what de Lauretis means when she
labels gender as both representation and its potential rupture or
trauma; for the double-bind here is that those elements not represented by the phallic signifier are only known by their representation as non-representational (I am being mimetic; the logic of
the phallus is as convoluted as the prose of this sentence).
Representation is origin – a dynamic which, from at least the time
of Plato, has been repressed. The trick of heterosexuality, the
means by which it propagates and sustains itself, is not so much
in what it says, but in how it says it. However, its more cunning
trick is in how it effaces this fact. By positing power as the
exercise of content, and not of form, it seduces us into replicating
its form even as we attempt to reject its content. And the replication of this form is, I claim, what we see in the positioning of the
body in *l'écriture féminine*. While disrupting the gender structure
of phallic ontology, *l'écriture féminine* replicates the signifying
dynamics that allow its sexual structure to remain intact.[8]

THE HOMOSEXUAL BODY

None of which, of course, is the distinctive or exclusive domain of French feminism. Indeed, in order to open our discussion to the full ramifications of specular mimesis – and so that we can escape its grasp – we must also recognize that male homosexual representation has just as often replicated the form of heterosexuality. One place to begin this recognition is with André Gide's *Corydon*. Written in the wake of the ground-breaking *Kulturkampf* movement of early German homosexual liberation,[9] invoking the authorizing presences of, among others, Whitman, Wilde, Ellis and Darwin,[10] and intertextually linked with Plato and Virgil through the dialogue form and the use of the names Corydon and Alexis,[11] Gide's four dialogues are frequently posited as the apotheosis of what we might be tempted to call an *écriture homosexual*. The forced neologism is particularly fitting here, for Gide's tracts also reinscribe the tropics of deferral and repression that I have claimed constitute the representational scene of heterosexuality.

As with the theorizations of Irigaray and Cixous, the tropics of deferral in Gide's writings are hidden behind what at first appears to be a radical destabilization. The initial strategy employed by Corydon is to undermine the idea of homosexuality as *contra naturam* by questioning the validity of nature as a heterosexual authority. The supremacy of heterosexuality because of its procreative ability is, according to Corydon, an *ex post facto* construct; nature, he says, sustains no such privilege:

> Nature constitutes a network without beginning or end, and who knows where to grasp this unbroken series of links; moreover, nothing remains more problematical than knowing if each link finds its *raison d'être* in the predecessor or in its successor (if indeed it has a *raison d'être* at all), and if the whole book of nature, to be properly understood, should not be read backward – in other words, if the last page is not the explanation of the first, the final link the secret motive of the beginning.
>
> (tr. Howard 50)

'Love' – by which I take Corydon to mean not simply love, but also its hierarchicalization into social representations such as good/procreative/heterosexual versus bad/sterile/homosexual

– 'is an entirely human invention – it does not exist in a state of nature' (33). Rather, the derogation against which Corydon must defend homosexuality is validated and imposed solely by its own representation:

> Just think how in our society, in our behavior, everything predestines one sex to the other; everything teaches heterosexuality, everything urges it upon us, everything provokes us to it: theater, literature, newspapers, the paraded example set by our elders, the ritual of our drawing rooms and our street corners . . . . Yet if a young man finally succumbs to so much collusion in the world around him, you refuse to grant that his decision was influenced, his desire manipulated if he ends up making his choice in the 'right' direction!
>
> (29)

To understand the radicality of this position, we might juxtapose it momentarily to the formulations of Hocquenghem and of a similar theorist, Felix Guattari. As Hocquenghem says, 'desire emerges in a multiple form, whose components are only divisible *a posteriori*, according to how we manipulate it' (*Homosexual Desire* 36). Explaining the philosophical underpinnings of *Anti-Oedipus*, Guattari has offered an almost identical formulation:

> Once desire is specified as sexuality, it enters into forms of particularized power, into the stratification of castes, of styles, of sexual classes . . . . [D]esire is everything that exists *before* the opposition between subject and object, *before* representation and production.
>
> (5)

Common to all of these positions is a notion of heterosexuality *not* as a natural expression, but as an intervention or re-representation. Gide's purpose, then, might be summarized by the title of Guattari's interview: to liberate (homosexual) desire, to separate it from the hierarchical constructions that typified early twentieth-century theories of inversion and pederasty.

But this liberation is only half of Gide's project. The second part of his strategy involves the reinscription of nature – albeit a different one – as the deferred authority of homosexual representation. Synthesizing the naturalist works of Remy de Gourmont, J. H. Fabre, Lester Ward and Charles Darwin, Corydon asserts that the phrase 'sexual instinct' is used 'to cover a bundle of automatisms or at least of tendencies which are solidly linked together in the lower species but which, as you ascend the steps of the animal ladder, become dissociated more and more easily and more and more frequently' (35), the result being that in 'higher species' 'pleasure is pursued for itself, without concern for fertilization' (36). Corydon summarizes the intent of such an argument early in the tract: 'The only thing in the world I concede as not natural is a work of art. Everything else, like it or not, belongs to the natural order' (20). Hocquenghem, who mentions Gide in passing, condemns such a strategy: 'attempts to construct a homosexuality which is biologically based, by means of a comparison with other species, [are] simply walking foolishly into the trap, which consists of a need to base the form of desire on nature' (*Homosexual Desire* 48) – but the terms of this critique need to be unpacked. It seems to me as if Gide is not 'trapped' into nature, but begins with it as an assumption. Then, by deconstructing the 'nature' that validates heterosexuality, Gide 'liberates' a space for desire. But in reconstructing homosexuality as natural, Gide reinscribes the very strategy that authorizes heterosexuality. Hence he is forced to relegate it to 'lower' species, and, in a masterful appropriation of Darwin, to posit it as the lower end of evolution.[12]

The point of this foray into Gide is to draw a structural parallel. In *l'écriture féminine*, meaning is exposed as being constructed by and constructive of a certain body that privileges the masculine, and then the female body is posited as an alternative origin. In Gide's theory, a construct of 'compulsory heterosexuality' is said to be constructing of and constructed by 'nature,' then another 'nature' is posited to validate homosexuality. The political appeal of such maneuvers cannot and should not be denied. They speak to that powerful and potent strategy of using the master's tools to break our own fetters. But in the process, something is also lost. For what we achieve in such maneuvers is difference *within* structures, not difference *to* them – as if we had simply changed apartments within the same tenement. I am compelled to ask in these instances if our gains are not a ruse, a staged 'impotency' on the part of heterosexual, male hegemony whereby we think we win even as we lose. What is at stake here is a question of authority, and in both cases it remains out of our hands. The body *behind* discourse empowers us; the nature coming *before* us makes us significant. Authority rests in a place that is always already gone, and we are forced to ignore the present moment as we look elsewhere. The tropics of deferral that underpin heterosexual representation and that continue to color the tactics of *l'écriture féminine* and Gide are not simply mimetic oddities; they are rather the exercise of power, the maintenance of the status quo through the relegation of the site of change to a place that is inaccessible and, supposedly, undeniable.

Can we speak differently? Can we maintain the authority of the body that *l'écriture féminine* has so importantly asserted, but in a way that does not reinscribe the tropics of deferral, and thereby also remove authority? If such a process is to be imagined, it must begin by activating the authority of representation and placing it firmly within the scene of representation. What I would like to do in the remainder of this argument is to suggest some ways in which male homosexual representation may be able to do this.

Dinky Adams, the male femme-fatale central to the urban epic quest of Larry Kramer's *Faggots*, provides us with a productive model for a poetics of the male homosexual body.

> Dinky Adams's ass was the first ass Fred had ever rimmed.
> He had, of course, heard about rimming. It was quite popular with some of the boys. But Fred had never wanted to so taste anyone before.

> And in he stuck his tongue into Dinky's asshole.
> He just did it. It tasted good. It tasted very good. It was smooth and clean, rather like a good quality moist satin. Dinky's asshole was lined with a lovely ribbon! (33)

> Jack . . . pushed his hand in a little. The fingers went in easily. Dinky, despite his claims to the contrary, must have been practicing. Yes, the fingers squidged in easily. A good thing I clipped my nails just this afternoon. Then the palm, bent in two as much as Jack could bend and squeeze it. Then, once inside the early walls, he clenched, ever so tightly, into the fist that gave this sport its name.

> So I am finally fist-fucking Dinky . . . .
> But then Laverne [Jack] realized that Dinky inside was so different from Dinky outside. Even with gobs of Crisco greasing the path, Jack could still feel the difference between Proctor & Gamble and Dinky. Dinky's insides were lined with lovely ribbons!
>
> (355–56)

At both the beginning and end of the novel Dinky's anus is the
threshold across which (or rather, *through* which) characters enter
new scenes of representation. Fred Lemish, the hero fixated
throughout the novel on the frequency and consistency of his
own bowel movements, suddenly finds in Dinky's ass 'an elegant
pillow in a perfect Italian palazzo' in which to bury his face (33).
Jack, also known as Laverne, feels compelled to sing in response
to the wonders of Dinky's anus: 'There's a new day coming and a
new world, too, here comes the sun, it's all right, going to be all
right' (356). And in each case the sexual acts are metaphorically
figured as bizarre transactions between the anal and the material;
for each man finds in Dinky's anus, not repulsion or even feces,
but ribbons (victory ribbons? hair ribbons? we do not know).

These acts are bizarre transactions in another way, for each
represents a negotiation between the public and the private. In
the case of Laverne's fist-fucking, the transaction is overt. The
opening of Dinky's most 'private' orifice happens not in the
'privacy' of a bedroom, but in the counter-culture amphitheater
of the meat-rack at Fire Island. Laverne stimulates Dinky, and the
gathered crowd is correspondingly gratified:

> Gasps of admiration from the crowd! Look at those doors
> open! That guy can really take it! Yes, gasps of admiration
> from the crowd!

> The crowd at least was most impressed. Gasps of empathy and
> admiration and hero-worship and the manifestation of same as
> fists shot up and clenched and reclenched like applause. Oh,
> heroes of old, ancient Greece and Rome, Thrace and Asia
> Minor, Crete and all points East and West, make way, make
> way, make way for Dinky Adams! Yes, gasps of pride for one
> of their own went up from all around.

(357–58)

In the case of Fred's rimming, the same boundaries are trans-
gressed on a more contained level. The experience is 'so gorgeous
that Fred's own cock became gigantic' (32). Similarly,

> Dinky was obviously enjoying it, because he was growing an
> even larger hard-on than any Fred had seen him grow during
> their times together, which had not always been the case,
> Dinky's hard-ons, which was something Fred didn't like to

think about or look at, as he now was looking at Dinky's own present giganticism.

(33)

Whatever else one might want to say about Dinky's anus, one thing is certain: it makes things look different. The 'privacy' of penetration becomes both congruent with and conducive to mass mob desire; the organ which should expel waste from the body now directs pleasure to the penis.[13]

The reconfiguration of materiality, privacy and the body that is signalled in these scenes also signals a mimesis – an *other-mimesis* – that contrasts with the strategies of heterosexual representation. The tropics of deferral and delay that typify heterosexuality are specified in and by a construction of the body that seeks to limit access to material power through a classification of organs across the binarism of public/private. As Hocquenghem has stated, the Oedipal pyramid, the structure through which the procreative phallus remains 'on top,' is achieved primarily through the privatization of other organs:

> Every man possesses a phallus which guarantees him a social role; every man has an anus which is truly his own, in the most secret depths of his own person. The anus does not exist in a social relation, since it forms precisely the individual and therefore enables the division between society and the individual to be made . . . . All libidinal energy directed towards the anus is diverted so that the social field may be organised along lines of sublimation and the private person.
>
> (*Homosexual Desire* 83)

The theorization here is important in two senses. First, it points out to us how the phallus (which, though not identical to the penis, is not necessarily different from it) guards access to materiality, to interaction in the social sphere. Second, it also demonstrates how the mimetic strategy used to empower the phallus also takes as its goal the construction of a stratified representation.[14] It is not simply the job of heterosexual representation to articulate the phallus; it is also its job to construct the space of deferral, the other to the represented phallus. The phallus needs to be public, therefore the anus is private; the phallus needs to have material power, therefore the anus is immaterial. Such a statement, of course, opens a problematic of causality. We might very well ask, to appropriate Abbott and Costello, who's on top – the phallus which controls public access, or the anus which allows this control through contradistinction.

The position ascribed to the anus within heterosexual phallic ontology is, therefore, not without a certain power. And this power seems to me to be liberated within the representational scene of Dinky's asshole. For in both of these episodes the pyramid of heterosexual deferral disappears. The private becomes the public, the immaterial is experienced materially, and the anus is no longer the antithesis to the phallus, but its complement. There is, as in *l'écriture féminine*, an investment in a bodily specificity in Kramer's representation. However, it is a representation that is unable to reach behind itself, for to do so is to touch precisely the heterosexual anus, an organ always posited as other to the actual scene of the phallus. Rather, Kramer's representation empowers itself by 'lifting' the anus into the scene (a maneuver requiring both physical and poetical dexterity). For the 'meaning' of these scenes derives not from the anus's association with deferred spaces of authority, but from its titillation and stimulation – its *activation* – in the present moment.

There is, of course, a caveat to be drawn here. For the difference of Kramer's representation depends on the traditional epistemology of the anus. That is, the power of activating the anus depends entirely on the fact that the anus is traditionally associated with inactivity, or with unauthorized, unvalorized activities such as defecation or deviant intercourse. But the point here is that the homosexual body in this representation unwrites the traditional hierarchies of deferral that empower the phallus. What is at stake here is not the content of representation, but its vectoring. This strategy is mimetically replicated throughout the novel in instances that seem at first unrelated to rimming and fist-fucking. Consider, for example, this tongue-in-cheek (pun intended) review of the etiology of homosexuality:

> . . . there's a current trend afoot attempting to indicate that homosexuality might be caused by genetic intrusions or embryonic hormonal imbalances, and there may be truth or succor found in this, or anything else the genes boys might come up with, and wouldn't it be nicer, easier, neater, cleaner, and certainly more convenient, if homosexuals were born just like everybody else? There is also that other school of thought,

established by S. Freud and his dishy disciples (including the
Messrs. Cult, Nerdley, Fallinger & Dridge), which posits that a
dumb dodo of a daddy and a whiz bang whammerino of a Ma
. . . can turn the trick as well.

(71)

Or this further elaboration:

Stander F. Lure, in his classic study of homosexuality, *The
Perversion of Mount Ararat* (which takes as its text the Biblical
maxim: ' . . . and the sons of Sennacherib shall rise up and
smoot the father of his own thing . . . '), has this to say: 'There
are certain instances when perversion develops from no
known cause – where parental figures have been accepted and
where roles have not been confused, where, in fact, there is no
reason at all obvious why the offspring should have emerged
warped and abnormal.'

(93)

The second example, based on a facetious maxim, comes to no
conclusion, and the first, setting at odds the equally inconclusive
polarities of nature and nurture, does nothing to further understanding. Clearly such 'authorities' offer no insight into the scene
of homosexuality; rather, their citation lampoons the desire for
external authority, for the need to base representation on some
already assumed object, whether it be the 'real' body, 'real'
nature, or S. Freud and his dishy disciples. The point behind such
satire seems to me to be the same one that Aaron Fricke makes in
his poignant memoir *Reflections of a Rock Lobster*: ' . . . it is as
impossible to explain why homosexuality exists as to explain
why heterosexuality exists . . . . Homosexuality *does* exist. And
now let's get on with the story' (8–9). Like the scenes of fisting
and rimming, which draw the body into the representational
scene rather than basing representation upon it, such formulations draw male homosexuality into the economy of the present
and refuse to relinquish it to the custody of totalizing diachronic
schema.

What is at stake in the debate I have staged here, then, is
precisely the difference Irigaray maps out between constitutive
and specular mimesis. For if Gide 'writes' the homosexual body
as the reflection of deferred authorities, Kramer writes it as the
mark of the here and now, as both the constructor of the present

and its index of power and effect. The importance of such a difference perhaps seems minimal in the campy context of Kramer's urban epic. However, its radical potentiality is fully exposed in Hocquenghem's 'literary' embodiment of his own theory, the novel *Love in Relief* [*L'amour en relief*]. Set in the epochal moment of France after the 1968 rebellion, the novel documents the experiences of Amar, a beautiful young man from the island of Kerkenna who is unexpectedly blinded in a scooter accident and forced to reassimilate himself into French culture. The relearning of the world is also a relearning of the body. While being bathed by Mrs Hallowe'en, a rich old woman who has befriended him, Amar reflects on the difference of his 'new' body:

> I had the tactile familiarity of my own body. When I was a little kid on Kerkenna, in the *hammam* (what you would call a Turkish bath) the masseur had twisted my arms and had climbed onto my back – in the midst of wooden pails filled with boiling water drawn from a steaming basin. Vapors ran along the platforms and climbed the columns toward the shadowy vaulted ceiling. I had learned the importance of the body from those long massages every Friday. Mrs. Hallowe'en had continued this ceremony in her own manner by sudsing me in the sunken tubs of intercontinental hotels.
>
> Unlike photography, there was no hidden sense in this activity. Everyone was equalized: I was completely mixed in with the sensual world.
>
> After a few lessons I could 'read' a body, and with my busy contented hands, work on sprains, cramps and other muscular weaknesses. Bodies trembled, became firm, admitted their frailties.
>
> (60)

We might find in this passage a parable for our own critical practice. As a blind person, Amar is privileged to a different set of representational assumptions: 'I was not in darkness but in a world without color, without shape, with the persistent impression of a simple fog just on the verge of breaking up' (29). Moreover, this different scene of representation allows a different 'use' of the body. Fully aware of the importance ascribed to the body by his culture (it has been 'impressed' on him by both masseurs and Mrs Hallowe'en), Amar can then use this knowledge in a *different* way – a way that refuses to privilege rifts between self and other, between the present and the past, or between the real and the imaginary: 'Everyone was equalized: I was completely mixed in with the sensual world.'

This representation is also other to the tropics of heterosexual deferral for, as Amar tells us, 'They cited Oedipus, Orpheus and a sorcerer named Tiresias, who once looked upon his goddess mother as she was bathing nude. I never desired my mother, not even in dreams' (29). The invocation of Oedipus seems overtly to mock Freud, and the continued questioning of the limits of the body seems to mock the Lacanian conception of the mirror stage. Other to sight, to the specular economy that, in heterosexual ontology, demands divisions between self and other and between object and image, Amar is energized fully in the present moment: 'so now I didn't know where the "I" stopped' (115).[15] For Amar, the domains of privatization and removal that typify the heterosexual body disappear; as he says, 'I didn't have a well-defined sense of ownership of my body' (123–24). Released from the need to base authority on external forces, Amar's relation to the 'real' also changes: 'The surface of the world turns toward me' (203). Moreover, this change in the vectoring of representation also allows Amar to perceive the dynamics of power and control implicit in specular mimesis:

> I never imagined how Mrs. Hallowe'en looked. The image of the image didn't excite me anymore, as had still happened on Kerkenna. The image of the image, the mental repetition of the word 'image,' whose secret I was trying to pierce by chanting aloud, just after the accident. As if to say 'colors,' or the names of colors, forms, of bodies, would make you master them.
>
> (62)

To be sure, Amar's transformation is not entirely to be desired. The loss of sight is significant, but it does allow Amar to recognize the power of a representation that is absolutely different, a representation that does not simply reflect differently, but constitutes difference.

WRITING WITH THE BODY

If I were to summarize the plea I have made in this discussion, it would be that we must learn to write *with* (the) body. The well-known phrase Americans have associated with *l'écriture féminine*, 'writing from/of the body,' already removes the body from the scene of writing and posits representation as after the fact. Writing *with* (the) body, in contrast, posits several meanings that contradict this notion: using the body as both the site and scribe of representation; allowing the body to exist concurrently with representation; representation validated by its own materiality, its own 'body,' rather than simply by its referentiality. Moreover, such a phrase allows us to recognize that power exists and affects us in the present tense, and, therefore, can be changed in the here and now. In such a practice, moreover, we are not writing with (the) body so much as we are writing with its odors, the effects of the body that can be perceived like smells, but that are never reified. Such a practice, therefore, allows us to assert the body without also stabilizing it or allowing 'the thing itself' unintentionally to validate other hierarchies of representation that also need to be skeptically interrogated. If writing from/of the body has allowed us to conceptualize the power of the body, writing with (the) body will allow us to liberate this power.

In short, if *l'écriture féminine* has asked us to find security in the body as *thing*, I am suggesting that we should find power in the body as *process*. We might think here of Sullivan, the pseudo-drag, pseudo-pandering, entirely camp orchestrator of Andrew Holleran's *Dancer from the Dance*: Sullivan, who reminds us that 'we live in a rude and dangerous time in which there are no values to speak to and one can cling only to concrete things – such as cock' (95); Sullivan, who responds to the existential queries of his friend Malone with 'We think too much! Blow my head off, darling, and leave me just a highly sensitized anus!' (138); Sullivan, who replies when asked what it means to be gay with the sage advice, 'Just repeat after me: "My face seats five, my honeypot's on fire"' (51). What Sullivan implicitly recognizes is that the security of stable truths pales in comparison to the wonders of the body in motion. And we can learn from this. For while by recognizing the body as process we at first surrender certain powers and authorities, we also might in the long run gain. We might find a way to assert gay men and lesbians as more than simply different by establishing the difference of everything. We might find a way of speaking the truth by recognizing that truth is false. We might find a way to our own essences by demonstrating that there is nothing essential. Such a project, asking as it does to recuperate 'identity' by abandoning what we currently mean by the term, is risky and unsettling. To calm our fears, let's repeat after me: my face seats five, my honeypot's on fire.

NOTES

1 The phrase I am picking up is taken from Gallop's critique of Barthes's style in his *Sade, Fourier, Loyola*: 'To choose fragmentation as a style is to erect a consistent defense against the body as insubordinate to man-made meanings' (18). My further argument will inevitably indicate that I disagree with Gallop's positioning of the body. However, her basic point that the representation of the body is always subject to other ruptures is important and complements my argument as a whole (see 11–20 passim.).

2 Readers approaching *l'écriture féminine* for the first time will want to consult Jones's two fine articles, 'Writing the Body: Toward an Understanding of *l'écriture féminine*,' and 'Inscribing Femininity: French Theories of the Feminine,' for cogent summaries of the movement. An interesting but more biased overview has been offered by Toril Moi in *Sexual/Textual Politics* (89–173). The feminist critique of *l'écriture féminine* had been set forth most powerfully by Christine Fauré's 'The Twilight of the Goddesses' and Carolyn Burke's 'Irigaray Through the Looking Glass.' For a summary of this critique, see Diana Fuss's *Essentially Speaking* (56–58), as well as Paul Smith's superlative summary and analysis of French feminisms in *Discerning the Subject* (133–52). Contrastingly, Domna C. Stanton's 'Language and Revolution' has offered an influential defense of Irigaray and Cixous and their importance to the Anglo-feminist scene.

3 I assume this project has reached the status of commonplace in feminist and gender theory; those unfamiliar with its basic terms will want to consult Teresa de Lauretis's *Feminist Studies/Critical Studies*, Stephen Heath's 'Difference,' Naomi Schor's 'Dreaming Dissymmetry,' and Gayatri Spivak's *In Other Worlds*.

4 The importance of Rubin's distinction has been further elaborated by Eve Kosofsky Sedgwick (*Epistemology*, 27–39; 'Across Gender,' 53–61).

5 All emphases in this and succeeding quotations are from the original unless otherwise noted.

6 Although I do not go into it here, Irigaray's formulation is especially distressing to the gay male theorist, because it implies that homosexual and homosocial behavior are the same. On the problematics of these two terms, see Eve Kosofsky Sedgwick, *Between Men* (1–20). For a perceptive analysis of the limits of Irigaray's ho(m)mo-sexuality, see Craig Owen's 'Outlaws' (223–24).

7 For a perceptive and accessible discussion of the importance of this passage to poststructural theory, see Jonathan Culler's *On Deconstruction* (86–89).

8 In a related argument about some of the repressions within Irigaray

and Cixous, Alice Jardine examines the silencing of women writers within these theories of woman's writing (*Gynesis*, 62–63, 261–62). Jardine's analysis would have to be slightly modified by Cixous's recent embrace of Clarice Lispector, but her argument is nonetheless compelling.

9 For detailed analyses of the German homosexual movement, see John Lauritsen and David Thorstad's *The Early Homosexual Rights Movement*, and James D. Steakley's *The Homosexual Emancipation Movement in Germany*. For a schematic but helpful overview of the early homophile movements in Germany, France, England and the United States, see Barry D. Adam's *The Rise of a Gay and Lesbian Movement* (17–44).

10 For a discussion of the 'sex-ology' of Ellis and its relationship to redefinitions of sexual subjectivity in the late 19th century, see David M. Halperin's *One Hundred Years of Homosexuality* (16–17).

11 For a discussion of the influence of Virgil and Theocritus on Gide's writings, see Jeffrey Meyers's *Homosexuality and Literature, 1890–1930* (37–38).

12 My critique of Gide, it should be noted, is in many ways unfair, in that it lifts his theory from its cultural milieu. Considering the time of its utterance (c. 1910), the tract is an amazingly visionary theorization. For the background of Gide and an interesting discussion of his life, see Justin O'Brien's *Portrait of André Gide*. For an alternative analysis of the second dialogue, see Frank Beach's commentary to the 1950 edition of *Corydon*.

13 Interestingly, *Faggots* was initially met with much hostility from the gay activist community on several counts. For an analysis of the place of *Faggots* within early 1980s American gay political culture, see Dennis Altman's *The Homosexualization of America* (180–88).

14 I discuss this idea in more detail in 'The Postmodernist and the Homosexual.'

15 The novel here, as well as much of Hocquenghem's theory in *Homosexual Desire*, interestingly presages Leo Bersani's analysis in 'Is the Rectum a Grave?' Consider, for example, the correlation between Amar's statements and Bersani's conclusion: 'Male homosexuality advertises the risk of the sexual itself as the risk of self-dismissal, of *losing sight* of the self, and in so doing it proposes and dangerously represents *jouissance* as a mode of ascesis' (222).

REFERENCES

Adam, Barry D. (1987) *The Rise of a Gay and Lesbian Movement*, Boston, Twayne.

Altman, Dennis (198) *The Homosexualization of America*, Boston, Beacon Press.

Bersani, Leo (1987) 'Is the Rectum a Grave?' *October* 43: 197–222.

Boston Women's Health Collective (1976) *Our Bodies, Ourselves: A Book by and for Women*, New York, Simon and Schuster.

Bredbeck, Gregory W. 'The Postmodernist and the Homosexual: A Dialogue' in Bill Readings and Bennett Schaber, eds, *Postmodernism Across the Ages*, Syracuse, Syracuse UP, forthcoming.

Burke, Carolyn (1981) 'Irigaray Through the Looking Glass,' *Feminist Studies* 7:2 (Summer): 288–306.

Cixous, Hélène (1981) 'The Laugh of the Medusa' in Elaine Marks and Isabelle de Courtivron, eds, *New French Feminisms: An Anthology*, New York, Schocken Books: 245–64.

Culler, Jonathan (1982) *On Deconstruction: Theory and Criticism after Structuralism*, Ithaca, Cornell UP.

De Lauretis, Teresa, ed. (1987) *Feminist Studies/Critical Studies*, Bloomington, Indiana UP.

—— (1987) *Technologies of Gender: Essays on Theory, Film, and Fiction*, Bloomington, Indiana UP.

Deleuze, Gilles and Felix Guattari (1983) *Anti-Oedipus: Capitalism and Schizophrenia*, trans. Robert Hurley, Mark Seem and Helen R. Lane, Minneapolis, U of Minnesota P, 1983.

Fauré, Christine (1981) 'The Twilight of the Goddesses, or the Intellectual Crisis of French Feminism,' *Signs* 7:1 (Autumn): 81–86.

Fricke, Aaron (1981) *Reflections of a Rock Lobster: A Story about Growing up Gay*, Boston, Alyson Publications.

Fuss, Diana (1989) *Essentially Speaking: Nature, Feminism, Difference*, New York, Routledge.

Gallop, Jane (1988) *Thinking Through the Body*, New York, Columbia UP.

Gide, André (1950) *Corydon*, trans. Frank Beach, New York, Noonday Press.

—— (1983) *Corydon*, trans. Richard Howard, New York, Farrar, Straus & Giroux.

Guattari, Felix (1979) 'A Liberation of Desire: An Interview by George Stambolian' in Elaine Marks and George Stambolian, eds, *Homosexualities and French Literature: Cultural Contexts/Critical Texts*, Ithaca, Cornell UP, 56–69.

Halperin, David M. (1990) *One Hundred Years of Homosexuality and Other Essays on Greek Love*, New York, Routledge.

Heath, Stephen (1978) 'Difference,' *Screen* 19:3: 50–112.

Hobbes, Thomas (1968) *Leviathan*. Ed. C. B. Macpherson, Harmondsworth, Penguin.

Hocquenghem, Guy (1978) *Homosexual Desire*, trans. Daniella Dangoor, London, Allison and Busby.

—— (1986) *Love in Relief*, trans. Michael Whisler, New York, SeaHorse Press.

Holleran, Andrew (1986) *Dancer from the Dance*, New York, New American Library.

Husserl-Kapit, Susan (1975) 'An Interview with Marguerite Duras,' *Signs* 1: 423–434.

Irigaray, Luce (1985) *Speculum of the Other Woman*, trans. Gillian C. Gill, Ithaca, Cornell UP.

—— (1985) *This Sex Which is Not One*, trans. Catherine Porter, Ithaca, Cornell UP.

Jardine, Alice A. (1985) *Gynesis: Configurations of Women and Modernity*, Ithaca, Cornell UP.

Jones, Ann Rosalind (1985) 'Inscribing Femininity: French Theories of the Feminine' in Gayle Greene and Coppelia Kahn, eds, *Making a Difference: Feminist Literary Criticism*, London, Routledge, 80–112.

—— (1985) 'Writing the Body: Toward an Understanding of *l'écriture féminine*' in Judith Newton and Deborah Rosenfelt, eds, *Feminist Criticism and Social Change: Sex, Class and Race in Literature and Culture*, New York, Methuen, 86–101.

Kramer, Larry (1978) *Faggots*, New York, New American Library.

Lauritsen, John and David Thorstad (1974) *The Early Homosexual Rights Movement*, New York, Times Change Press.

Meyers, Jeffrey (1977) *Homosexuality and Literature, 1890–1930*, Montreal, McGill–Queen's UP.

Moi, Toril (1985) *Sexual/Textual Politics: Feminist Literary Theory*, London, Routledge.

Nietzsche, Friedrich (1966) *Werke*. Ed. Karl Schlechta, Munich, Hanser, 3 vols.

O'Brien, Justin (1953) *Portrait of André Gide: A Critical Biography*, New York, McGraw.

Owens, Craig (1987) 'Outlaws: Gay Men in Feminism' in Alice Jardine and Paul Smith, eds, *Men in Feminism*, New York, Methuen, 219–32.

Plato (1951) *The Symposium*, trans. Walter Hamilton, Harmondsworth, Penguin.

Rubin, Gayle (1984) 'Thinking Sex: Notes for a Radical Theory of the Politics of Sexuality' in Carole S. Vance, ed., *Pleasure and Danger: Exploring Female Sexuality*, Boston, Routledge, 307–8.

Schor, Naomi (1987) 'Dreaming Dissymmetry: Barthes, Foucault, and Sexual Difference' in Alice Jardine and Paul Smith, eds, *Men in Feminism*, New York, Methuen, 98–110.

Sedgwick, Eve Kosofsky (1985) *Between Men: English Literature and Male Homosexual Desire*, New York, Columbia UP.

—— (1989) 'Across Gender, Across Sexuality: Willa Cather and Others' in Ronald R. Butters, John M. Clum, and Michael Moon, eds, *Displacing Homophobia: Gay Male Perspectives in Literature and Culture*, Durham, Duke UP, 53–72.

—— (1990) *The Epistemology of the Closet*, Berkeley, U California P.

Smith, Paul (1988) *Discerning the Subject*, Minneapolis, U Minnesota P.

Spivak, Gayatri Chakravorty (1987) *In Other Worlds: Essays in Cultural Politics*, New York, Methuen.

Stanton, Domna C. (1986) 'Language and Revolution: The Franco-American Dis-Connection' in Hester Eisenstein and Alice Jardine, eds, *The Future of Difference*, Boston, G. K. Hall, 73–87.

Steakley, James D. (1975) *The Homosexual Emancipation Movement in Germany*, New York, Arno Press.

Wilde, Oscar (1989) *The Complete Works of Oscar Wilde*. Ed. J. B. Foreman, New York, Harper and Row.

Chapter 6

What do men want?

John Forrester

We should not forget the forces unleashed by the very act of constituting groups, of falling in with the social world's classificatory devices: men, women and so forth. The constitution of male groups was quite evidently always accompanied by, and often if not always emotionally predicated upon, the exclusion of women; at the very same time, those women were brought back and placed on a pedestal at the heart of the group. Women have nearly always been placed on pedestals by traditional all-male groups, from London clubs to rugby clubs, even if at the foot of the pedestal *Woman* there is always also her double, the infinitely degradable woman: the whore with a heart of gold, the miasmic source of infinite pleasure and disgust, the female orifice that opens onto reabsorption by whatever primeval slimes the male imagination can construct. And, of course, although there are some advantages to being on pedestals, the disadvantages are notorious. Not least amongst them is the fact that the man who idealizes the woman thereby infantilizes himself. Whence the astute comment of Brigid Brophy: 'I refuse to consign the whole male sex to the nursery. I insist on believing that some men are my equals.'

All-women clubs may also construct such phantasmagorical images. Let me quote the words of a dear friend of mine, a lesbian feminist who, some twelve years ago, described a close male friend of hers as 'the sort of hanger-on of feminist groups who always wants to be underneath.' Her pithy phrase provokes two reflections on my part: firstly, that all groups are subject to a version of the Groucho Marx principle. Instead of 'Any club that would accept me as a member, I wouldn't want to join,' the revised version runs: 'Anyone who wants to join my club I wouldn't want to have.' The male feminist hanger-on is viewed by his radical feminist friend not only with the suspicion that goody-goodies always provoke for wanting to be on the side of the angels, not only with the suspicion that he might be a fellow-traveller lured by the radical chic that has traditionally accompanied, in certain circles, any radically oriented sociopolitical grouping, but also with the sense that the last thing she wants is a man who conforms to what she says a man should be if he wants to join her group.

The domain of sexuality is full of contradictions of this sort, between moral ideals on the one hand and nasty shameful desires on the other. As Woody Allen puts it, 'Does sex have to be dirty? Yes, if it's done right.' The joke points to at least one happy solution to the problem of sex: namely, the possibility of being dirty and not minding, of escaping the codes of shame through 'good-enough coming,' to adapt Winnicott's notion of good-enough mothering.[1] But my friend seemed rather to be saying, 'The only sort of man who deserves the name is the man who wants to be on top, who both sexually and socially wishes to dominate, penetrate, be active, be in control. But that is precisely the sort of man I want nothing to do with.'

My second reflection on this story means asking a question more from the man's point of view. Is his desire to be a good feminist man really a desire to be underneath, to be dominated sexually, socially and politically by the feminist women he admires? Is his desire a kind of masochism, or a kind of fascination with the all-powerful woman figure, perhaps even with the phallic mother?

Having made these preliminary remarks, I want to return to the question 'What do men want?' and its psychoanalytic resonances. Freud originally, in 1931, asked the question 'What do women want?' to which mine is a counter.[2] His was not a question based on innocence or inexperience, but nor was it one he'd been asking himself for a long time. Rather, the question itself was the product of other findings. Freud had been working with women in the 1890s, women patients he called hysterics. In particular, he had isolated an important form of defence: hysterical identification. In hysterical identification the subject identifies with another person or thing on the basis of a common characteristic.[3] His account of hysterical symptom-formation was thus that the subject produced the symptoms appropriate to his being someone else: the symptom thus became the sign, the commemoration of the identification. Hence, in Dora's analysis, Dora's furious reaction to Herr K.'s remark, 'I have nothing from my wife,' stemmed from the damage this statement did to her identification with Frau K.: Dora was not angry that he attempted to seduce her by indicating how his desire for her was bound up with his empty marriage, but because he revealed that the woman with whom she identified felt no desire.[4] Similarly, Dora's giving Freud two weeks' notice suggested that she identified one, if not both of them, with the governess who had been seduced and abandoned by Herr K.[5] Note how seemingly 'normal' states, such as righteous anger, are treated by Freud as structured like symptoms, as the products of identification.

So when you want to find out what desire an hysteric is expressing through his or her symptom, you ask the question: 'With whom is he or she identifying?' This is the method which Freud set out in Dora's analysis – peeling off one by one the successive layers of her identification. In later Freudian theory and practice, this procedure then became the model for the overall procedure in the analysis not only of symptoms, but of the ego itself, for identification is the path by which the ego is constituted.[6] This similarity is good prima-facie evidence for Lacan's contention that the ego is the neurotic symptom *par excellence*: the model for the Freudian ego is the hysterical subject. Just as with hysterical symptoms, so with the ego: identifications are the permanent records of the love-relations the subject has experienced. Hence psychoanalysis, finding out what you desire, amounts to finding out whom you have identified yourself with – the history of those you have loved. For example, the one sentence the Wolf Man repeatedly uttered, 'I can't go on living like this,' was the key to a profound identification with his mother, who used to make this declaration to him when he was very young.[7]

Freud developed a theory in which this identificatory form of defense was contrasted with obsessional defenses. Briefly, obsessional defenses involve self-reproaches, attacks upon the self, for perverse sexual desires or memories. Whereas the hysteric abdicates responsibility for her desires by becoming someone else, the obsessional imprisons himself for being who he is. The world of the obsessional is a prison in which others have been eliminated, for fear of their being destroyed, used, raped, murdered by the subject. The world of the hysteric is a world of the desires of other people, in which the subject is submerged and lost in the theatre of other people's demands, desires and reproofs. There is a strong continuity in Freud's thought here, since he early on contrasts the female hysteric with the male obsessional, roughly along the lines I'm outlining here: the hysteric is too engaged with social reality, too subject to disappearing beneath the desire of the other, whereas the male obsessional has never entered a truly social world for fear of appearing as an aggressive perverse monster who will be punished. Later, Freud will recognize the ultimate fear generative of primal anxiety of the female to be the fear of loss of love; for the male, this fear will be called castration anxiety. In other words, the (phobic) male loves his penis in the same way that the (hysteric) female loves the hoped for penis-child which is what she loves her father for. The female fears loss of love to the same extent that the male fears loss of his penis.

So Freud's question, 'What do women want?' was both a continuation of his previous thinking and a new departure. For him, the neurosis of women always expressed the female subject's dispersion in the world of her objects, for the female was characterized by her intersubjective conflict, by the radical hiddenness of her desires and her objects, in contrast with the male, always caught in an intrasubjective conflict. Yet this account made the development of femininity a problem: it made it simply a matter of identification with the other, which is only a matter of postponing the problem, not of solving it. The same problem arises, incidentally, for all social role theories: if gender is simply the imprint of a social role, then I am obliged to ask the question of where the social role came from, *ad infinitum*, until I reach some answer which lies beyond the social.

Freud's question, however, did not just express his view of femininity as the plaything of the other, but also expressed a recognition of women's rock-like resistance to recognizing their love towards their earliest love-objects, their mothers. Freud's lack of concern for questions of gender was imperceptibly, but finally rudely, shaken by the discovery of the asymmetry of the development of the little girl from loving a mother to loving a man, as compared with the little boy, who retains his love of his mother under a variety of guises in loving a woman. And Freud was perplexed at how difficult women found it to acknowledge their love for their mothers.[8] The female subject often seemed to say, 'If becoming a woman means becoming like my mother, then I refuse it.' Women seem to refuse their primary love-object in a manner that is unimaginable to men; yet they are perpetually dissatisfied with the secondary objects to which they then turn, in disappointment, anger, sadness or revenge. Hence, the question: 'What do women want?' Hysterical identification in its pure form is no answer, because all it implies is the simple taking on board of the desires of another person: it doesn't tell one why the hysteric (or the ego) prefers to be someone else, prefers to desire what the other desires.

What do men want? A snappy answer would be: the penis, and a safe place to put it; crucially, the very notion of the 'safe place' would be guaranteed by mother. But what of the other question hidden behind 'What do men want?': 'What is a man?' Can we answer this by asking: with whom does a man identify? The answer seems straightforward: daddy. And it also seems clear that little boys have less difficulty identifying with their fathers than girls have in identifying with their mothers. Perhaps it is the facility with which men identify with their fathers, and with other seemingly unambiguous 'masculine' figures, which seems so disquieting to women, and to men who listen to the disquiet of women. Yet, now that we have asked the question, does that mean that the straightforward 'daddy' answer is becoming, under present cultural conditions, untenable, in the same way that women's identifications with their mothers was found by Freud to be problematic?

Let me be a little less abstract. When asked, 'What do men want?' one woman I know said: 'Men want their mothers – and power.' There was a little pause before she said the word 'power.' I heartily agree – men want their mothers, and when the consequences sink in, they need something to fend off the threat of absorption and being devoured that the image of the mother almost immediately evokes. They need power to reverse the helpless dependency which they experience when they have got what they want – mummy. So power comes next, to keep mummy under control, to retain their independence. And power also assures them that they are like daddy, who seemed to be able to love mummy and yet not be devoured, or destroyed. But 'having' mummy, and having a certain power so as to fend off feelings of dependency, doesn't always work. The next step is to limit the dependency by being contemptuous of what one is fearful of being dependent on – hence misogyny. And the final step is to split the mother figure into two: virgin and whore, or in less religious language, wife and mistress, or even mother and child. A more power-oriented account, a more social historical account would call this the strategy of divide and rule. One of the aims of this process is to secure a safe arena, that 'safe place,' for the expression of phallic sexuality, while at the same time preserving the mother image unsullied and intact, and evading confrontation with the anxiety that maternal desire may elicit. The penis here functions as a litmus paper for the paths chosen: on the one hand, as an index of the domain to be left untouched, a domain of maximal danger; on the other, as a sign of control and ascendancy over the mutilated others, those women for whom the expression of concern, sympathy, and tenderness may even become possible.

This pattern seems uneventful, unmysterious and stable. I want to make two further remarks about it. Firstly, one of the obvious reasons for its stability is the manner in which it links up the aim of preserving the mother intact with the reproduction of the species – the production of the babies, which is not only a way of keeping property in the family, but is also a very good way of further safeguarding one's primary narcissism. Nonetheless, it produces its fair share of casualties, even on the male side of things. Secondly, its structure may not be all that specific to men: after all, the account I have given says that men want their mothers. The Freudian starting point for an account of female sexuality is exactly the same: the pre-Oedipal relation of girls to their mothers, from which they have such difficulty in detaching themselves. The psychoanalytic question then becomes: how is it that women can detach their affections from their mothers, from their own sex, and transfer it to men? The answer is: if they ever do, which is by no means all that common, they do so by repudiation of their mothers out of despair, hatred and resentment. But the despair, hatred and resentment that the original relation to the mother undergoes is not that different for boys. They too must give up their mothers; but in their case, they do so out of fear, a more straightforwardly passive emotion, an emotion that embodies power relations in a more naked fashion. But for the psychoanalyst, the male too is highly unlikely to give up this primary relation to the mother: all he will do in the most ideal of cases is to displace his affection onto another woman, just like his mother. Indeed, in one of Freud's most moving passages, he describes how, in effect, the male's fear is displaced onto a third female figure: death. The ideal type of the man, then, will have 'three inevitable relations . . . with a woman – the woman who bears him, the woman who is his mate and the woman who destroys him . . . the mother herself, the beloved one chosen after her pattern, and lastly the Mother Earth who receives him once more.'[9]

But I now want to focus on one of the casualties of the process of defense against the all-powerful mother: perverts. This rather archaic term is still a useful one. We still need a term to capture the sense of outrage that we all feel about the sex lives of other people. As Somerset Maugham put it, 'My own belief is that there is hardly anyone whose sexual life, if it were broadcast, would not fill the world at large with surprise and horror.' In addition, it is useful to describe people who are unaccountably attached to specific sexual practices, often to the exclusion of others. I do not wish to have to define the term 'perversions' beyond this: suffice it to say that my list includes sadism, masochism, necrophilia, coprophilia, fetishism, rape, pedophilia, exhibitionism, voyeurism and going to the cinema. What is interesting about these practices is the fact that the vast majority of practitioners are men. Indeed, following a classical psychoanalytical mode of argumentation, I might propose that we could best give an answer to the question, 'What do men want?' by rephrasing it as, 'What do perverts want?' That might well be the best way into the thorny question of the nature of masculinity: assume that perversion is the purest expression of masculine sexuality. One of the curious consequences of this way of looking at male as it differs from female sexuality is that we may arrive at an answer as to what men (extrapolating from perverts) want once we discover why men are so much more committed to the practice of perversions than women are.

Well, what do men who practice the perversions want? Interestingly enough, perversion also arises from a crisis in the development of separation from the mother, or rather from a difficulty in accepting the primary identification with the mother. According to Robert Stoller, it arises from a combination of rage at having to give up the bliss of being cared for by the mother, fear of being trapped in her orbit, and a desire for revenge for her having put one in this predicament.[10] This theory goes hand in hand with a view of perversion as an arena for the expression of hostility to the other. But the expression of this hostility may take many forms, including that of the dialectic of the impersonal and the unique. As Masud Khan puts it, 'the pervert puts an impersonal object between his desire and his accomplice; this object can be a fantasy, a gadget or a pornographic image'.[11] One leg of the dialectic of sexual love is the aim of realizing the universal and general in the unique and particular: this woman, this man, this boy, embodies the general woman, man, boy, so that the sexual act between a man and a woman is a project of universal love between men and women. As John Berger points out, the desire to see the specific other naked is a desire to see that the other is just like all the others, that *this* woman is just a woman.[12] But the next move of the dialectic points to the unique and individual, and it is here that perversion comes to the fore: through the gadget or fantasy, the accomplice is alienated from the possibility of his embodying the universal, and becomes part of the project to embody the unique and singular. In becoming an extension of an object, in becoming an object for the subject, he may realize an aesthetic ideal of the unique object, rather than an ethical ideal of a sexual subject; he may become like a Leonardo or a Mapplethorpe, rather than the specific instantiation of a lover or a man.[13] The testing of limits in perversion, then, is the testing of the limits placed on the unique by the universal. Going to extremes of pain, discovering excesses beyond satiation, these are ways of exploring the limits of the unique in defiance of the exigencies of our ideal of a universal humanity.

Thinking along these lines has led some writers on erotism – Bataille, Sartre and Lacan are clear examples[14] – to view perversion as the privileged arena for the expression of a hostility which is struggling to remain within the limits of the human. Neither these French writers, nor Stoller or most of his fellow psychoanalysts, would contrast the hostility of perversion with a supposed benign neutrality, or pacific tone, of 'normal' sexual relations. Rather, their interest in the perversions frequently stems from the often direct confrontation they stage between sexual desire and death. Hence, the argument runs, the perversions represent a defiant challenge to, or at least an attempted exploration of, the biological and metaphysical fate of humans, in which sexuality and death are inextricably linked. We might surmise that women's sexuality presents them with a related metaphysical challenge: even today, we need no reminder that childbirth and death are intimately linked both in reality and in the imagination. One might even draw the link, with Freud and, surprisingly, with Masters and Johnson as well, between the female orgasm and childbirth.[15]

For men as well, the production of a child may conceal or mediate the manner in which sexuality implicates our own mortality. The child holds our mortality at bay through the narcissistic image that it revives. As Freud wrote in summarizing one of his dreams, 'And after all, I reflected, was not having children our only path to immortality?'[16] Perversion attempts to dispense with such a narcissistic screen, since it often goes beyond the reassurance of the narcissistic other, in quest of a more 'real,' more 'present' other, one more vulnerable and corporeal, one less directly dependent on the promise of the future. Perversion hopes to explore pathways other than those of replication, reproduction, or mirroring; it seeks an alternative to these latter sublimated modes of defense in which a narcissistic version of paternity – with its temptation to the father of reviving his own boyhood as a model of paternity – stands in for masculinity.

But it is also clear that the masculine hegemony on the perversions gives men a more intimate relation to explicit sexual hostility. With women, sexual hostility may well be expressed in more subtle forms, not only as masochism, that rather worn-out, catch-all term for whatever painful destinies are women's, but other, more socially acceptable forms of hostility. We are familiar with one such form: the pity that is the distorted expression of sadistic impulses. The revival of interest in the logic of seduction, which has so often been seen as a privileged arena of women's desires, from Baudrillard's essay[17] to Christopher Hampton's version of *Les liaisons dangereuses*, has also made us attentive to viewing seduction as a theater in which base aggression, hostility and all that is socially subversive and existentially defiant can be played out. For instance, one of the oldest tricks in the seducer's trade, playing the wounded little boy, elicits in the woman the 'hostile' impulse of caring and of making the wound go away, hostile in the sense that it involves a sizeable measure of controlling and of effacing pain. Nor should one underestimate the measure of aggression that it takes for a woman to don the maternal role. It is perhaps this achievement of supplanting, elbowing aside and maybe even robbing the mother that forms the ground for the question, 'What do women want?' and which may make it so difficult for them to answer. For men, the dangerous maternal space is always outside, so that the anxiety associated with the omnipotent and omni-devouring mother will coalesce around castration, even in its pre-Oedipal forms. But for women, the dangerous maternal space is also potentially within. The theme of robbing the mother's insides, so important in Melanie Klein's account of attaining a stable relationship to the mother's maternal functions, is crucial to the constitution of the woman's own body as maternal, with a confusion between ego-limits and body-limits, both depending on the answer to the question, 'Is there an inside to me?'[18]

Now we see that the position of men and women is not that different: for both, the sources of sexual hostility and anxiety arise from the common ground of the relation to the mother. In men, the crisis of identification comes when they feel that something fragile and hard won is threatened: Freud called it castration anxiety. In women, the crisis of identification lies in what it will cost to achieve an identification with the mother. Yet I want to end on another, more doubtful note.

Somewhere Freud notes: 'The deepest of all the child's yearnings is for the love and the protection that only a father can give.'[19] He certainly had as the background for this thought the great weight of protection that is a basic theme of the monotheistic religions. In recent decades, many have seen these caring and protecting functions as synonymous with motherhood and mothering. Of course, there are movements to widen the class of those who mother, so we now call the function that of 'parenting.' Such semantic generosity, however, goes hand in hand with an abdication of serious thinking about the distinctively paternal function. Both Reich and Lacan saw the form of modern neurosis and anxiety as stamped by a decline of the paternal function.[20] The more recent attacks on patriarchy and its embodiment in the bourgeois father figure of the recent past, the attacks on male domination in so many spheres of social life give the impression that the paternal function will from now on always elicit suspicion and mistrust.

Psychoanalytic theory has shifted with this trend. In Klein's theory, there is virtually no function for the father, save as part of a united parental couple that excludes the child.[21] In Winnicott and others, mother–child relations dominate the theory.[22] Yet the acquisition of gender involves giving body to the difference between the sexes. The function of father seems threatened to degenerate into an empty symbolic one: 'Daddy? Oh, he supplied the sperm. But we're both parents, you know.' As if non-gendered parents were more important, socially safer than the forbidden gendering of mummy and daddy. This accent on parents thus carries on by other means the general exclusion of the child from the sexed world of daddy and mummy, it repeats that staple of post-Oedipal psychic security, the delusion that parents never have sexual intercourse, the belief that parents do not take enjoyment in the genitals of the opposite sex, especially not their own.

By contrast, in both Freud and Lacan, it is the father who introduces the mystery of sexual difference in the form of a question the child puts to him or herself: 'There is something that Mummy receives from Daddy (or that someone else, that mother's other) that I can't give her or that she doesn't want from me. What is it?' This account of the Oedipal triangle might seem to explain one easy way for a man to identify with the father: since the father's function remains always mysterious, almost empty, identifying with it means simply taking up a distinctive position of giving a woman what she wants, but allowing her to specify what that is. This might well be the solution for our hanger-on feminist man: he wants to be wanted, and allows himself (I almost said his penis) to be what the woman wants. But identifying himself and the paternal function with his penis is no real solution. No doubt it is one that is often tried, by men who think that it is their sexual task, their sexual assignment, even their sexual vocation and duty, to satisfy the desire of a woman. But this version of the little boy's eager, tail-wagging desire to give mummy exactly what he imagines daddy gives her is too close to Don Juan's ideal for the feminist man to sustain for long. In reality, the paternal function is more mysterious than that, for both sexes. But it may still be true that both the questions, 'What do men want?' and 'What do women want?' are closely tied up with the answers children in general find to the question: 'What does mummy want?'

NOTES

1 Winnicott, D. W., 'True and False Self' (1960) in *Maturational Processes and the Facilitating Environment* (London: The Hogarth Press and the Institute of Psychoanalysis, 1965) 140–52.

2 Undated letter to Marie Bonaparte, quoted in Ernest Jones, *Sigmund Freud: Life and Work* (London: Hogarth, 1953–7), vol. II 468 (UK edition), vol. II 421 (US edition).

3 Sigmund Freud, 'Group psychology and the analysis of the ego,' in Freud, *The standard edition of the complete psychological works of Sigmund Freud*, Strachey ed., 24 vols (London: Hogarth and the Institute of Psychoanalysis, 1953–74), vol. XVIII 69–143.

4 Freud, 'A fragment of the analysis of a case of hysteria' (1905) SE VIII 7–121; Jacques Lacan, 'Intervention on transference' in *In Dora's Case, . . .* ed. C. Bernheimer and C. Kahane (New York: Columbia UP, 1985); and Juliet Mitchell and Jacqueline Rose, eds., *Feminine Sexuality: Jacques Lacan and the Ecole Freudienne*, trans. Jacqueline Rose, London: Macmillan, 1982.

5 See Lisa Appignanesi and John Forrester, *Freud's Women* (London: Weidenfeld and Nicolson; New York: Basic Books 1992).

6 Freud, *The ego and the id* (1923) SE XIX 7–23.

7 Freud, 'From the history of an infantile neurosis' (1914/18) SE XVII 26.

8 Freud, 'Female sexuality,' SE XXI 225–43.

9 Freud, 'The theme of the three caskets' (1913) SE XII 301.

10 Robert Stoller, *Perversion: The Erotic Form of Hatred* (London: Harvester, 1976), 99.

11 M. Masud Khan, *Alienation in Perversions* (London: Hogarth, 1979), 9.

12 John Berger, *Ways of Seeing* (Harmondsworth: Penguin, 1984), 59.

13 See the remarkable case history in Khan, Masud, 'The Evil Hand' in *Hidden Selves: Between Theory and Practice in Psychoanalysis*, London: Hogarth, 1983, 139–180.

14 Georges Bataille, *L'Erotisme* (Paris: Editions de Minuit, 1957); Jean-Paul Sartre, *Being and Nothingness*, trans. Hazel Barnes (New York: Philosophical Library, 1956); Jacques Lacan, 'Kant avec Sade' in *Ecrits* (Paris: Seuil, 1966).

15 See Freud, 'The economic problem of masochism' SE XIX 162: 'masochistic phantasies . . . place the subject in a characteristically female situation; they signify, that is, being castrated, being copulated with, or giving birth [*Kastriertwerden, Koitiertwerden oder Gebähren* {Stud III 346}].' On Masters and Johnson, see their account of the female orgasm, in *Human Sexual Response* (Boston: Little and Brown, 1966) 116–134, where they state that both by the women's own avowal, and according to their physiological data, certain stages of childbirth are indistinguishable from the sensations of orgasm.

16 Freud, *The Interpretation of Dreams*, SE V 487.

17 Jean Baudrillard, *De la séduction* (Paris: Flammarion, 1979).

18 See, for example, Melanie Klein, 'The psycho-analytic play

technique: its history and significance' (1955) in Melanie Klein, *Envy and Gratitude and other works, 1946–1963*, vol. III of *The Writings of Melanie Klein*, Roger Money-Kyrle, ed., 4 vols. (London: The Hogarth Press and the Institute of Psychoanalysis, 1975), 133.

19 Freud, *Group psychology and the analysis of the ego*, SE XVIII 69–143.

20 Wilhelm Reich, *The Mass Psychology of Fascism*, trans. Carfagno (New York: Penguin, 1978); Lacan, 'La famille' in *Encyclopédie Française* 1938 T. VIII, 'La Vie Mentale', reprinted as *Le complexe familiel* (Paris: Navarin, 1984). This reference is to 1938 edition, 8.40 – 16.

21 See Klein, 'Early stages of the Oedipus conflict and of super-ego formation' in Klein, *The Psychoanalysis of Children*, vol. II of *The Writings of Melanie Klein*, 132–3.

22 Winnicott, *The Child, the Family and the Outside World* (Harmondsworth: Penguin, 1964).

Part III

Between men: finding their own way

Chapter 7

Men and change

Reflections from a men's group

Vic Blake, Andy Brown, Robin Fairbairns, Bill Shephard, David Spiegelhalter, Martin Steckelmacher and Willie Sugg

The Cambridge Men's Group, whose thoughts and feelings make up this article, is of random origin and loose composition – as are the thoughts and feelings themselves. Our aim here is to offer some of the reflections we have shared on our experiences of being men. Although the loose structure of our presentation doesn't lend itself to firm conclusions, it typifies the style we have found most valuable in our approach to personal development and change.

We are a group of men who have met regularly over the last seven years. Our common ground when we started was our need for male friendship and support. New members gathered over the years, predisposed through personal need or radical orientation, and the seven current members now meet fortnightly. Other men are associated with the group through open meetings, or by being previous regular members, and we have sometimes helped them to set up other men's groups, as well as joined in national men's events. Although our white middle-class backgrounds are somewhat similar, we range in age from thirty-something to sixty, and no two of us are the same in anything but our gender. As we shall see later, our range of sexual orientation has become apparent as the group has developed.

When we started as a group in 1984 we had no well-formed analysis of the direction men should take in the light of feminism. We were guided, rather, by a mutual recognition of our own need for personal change and our need for support in order to achieve it. This realization has defined the structure of the present essay. Its four main sections progress through areas on which we've worked over the years: men in the world, men in the family, men as partners, and men as themselves. The order of the sections is significant: we find some things easier to work on than others, with the analysis of our own self-awareness being the most difficult of all. The length of the sections reflects the time given in our meetings to each issue – regardless of the 'importance' of the issues covered. For example, although we all find sex, sexuality, and 'coming out' important (and sometimes fun!), we tend not to discuss them repeatedly, while issues concerning families, work, and our general daily lives get worked over again and again. Following the fourth section, we present as a coda a brief view of our relationship to feminism and the women's movement.

The way in which this piece was written is an example of how we organize ourselves. We agreed upon a broad list of topics at a meeting, and everyone came back with written contributions. These were arranged by topic, and then a series of editorial meetings attended by various members led to the essays slowly taking shape. The final result comprises only about one-quarter of the original material, but this has not been the consequence of any individual exercising editorial control.

Before dealing with specific issues concerning men, we examine how our group operates in its regular meetings.

THE GROUP

We are deliberately leaderless, and although this means that we suffer from an occasional lack of direction, we feel this is easily counterbalanced by our joint responsibility for all that happens. We have settled upon a size of seven members at the moment, with a turnover of at most one or two a year. As a closed group, we often have to deal with requests of individual men who wish to be in a group. As we can't take in all who would like to join, we occasionally hold open meetings to encourage new groups to start.

> Over six years we have grown to a size that feels comfortable. With only four or five the group seemed too small to work well. One person missing a meeting disrupted continuity. At seven we feel we are not too big. We miss people, but don't need everyone at every meeting; we have a diffuse enough range of opinions and ideas that we don't get too bogged down or self-congratulatory.

Each meeting has a similar format beginning with a 'news and goods' introductory section of indeterminate length in which each member talks in turn about anything that has concerned them personally since we last met.

Each of us provides an update on our lives each time we meet. It is a great privilege to be allowed to follow these stories, year after year, through disappointments, joy, sadness, anger. The lives I hear about are far more interesting than any soap opera, and would, I am sure, be considered ludicrously far-fetched if they appeared as fiction.

And the next episode will be on Thursday next, same time, same place. The cycle ride to the group has been invaluable in working out which news to impart. At times I have felt quite embarrassed to say, 'Everything seems fine at the moment.'

Talking about the trivialities of my life to willing listeners – what a treat!

There is usually some idea from previous meetings for a discussion to fill the rest of the meeting, but often an immediate problem or worry strikes a chord in all of us, or someone has asked in 'news and goods' for more time, and we go on from there.

In the group there is little competition. We are all in the group because we are trying to avoid traditional male posturing, and we feel we have learnt that opening up, acknowledging our weaknesses and our fears, can make us stronger rather than weaker. The group acts as a mechanism to enable men to talk freely to each other.

Time has made me realize the importance of being able to talk about how I feel. Often it is only after spontaneously talking about a relationship that I realize my true feelings about the other person.

One of our recurring determinations is to create an atmosphere in which conflict could be expressed and gone through. But we are also aware of our unwillingness to criticize each other: our concern for mutual support almost gets in the way.

I have always found confrontation extremely difficult and upsetting. I know there has been some change in my attitudes, in that I now have a greater belief that conflict can be acknowledged and, if not resolved, that at least it does not necessarily mean the rejection of all communication. We are probably much too soft with each other, but maybe I prefer it that way.

Sometimes I have been frustrated by the lack of confrontation and challenge within the group – but I have been frequently surprised and relieved by our tolerance.

The group is certainly more than the sum of its parts – initially resisting newcomers, mourning departures, playing safe, falling out – and generally well-motivated to see mutual support as the key task.

The group helped me to see what I did not like about that job and to leave it – one of the best moves of my life.

Introspection and self-reflection can be fun and is often hilarious. Hitherto I'd thought it deeply serious, difficult and painful.

The strength of the men's group is that we have no ready answers. The process of sharing and trying to understand the confusions in our lives does more than explaining them.

MEN IN THE WORLD

A group that has continued for so long cannot just deal with single 'political' issues: the group becomes an integral part of all our lives, and our daily lives are reflected back to the group. We are trying, with mixed success, to change how we are in all aspects of how we live, and it is natural to begin with the familiar territory of men – the outside world of work. This leads on to how we behave and feel with other men, and finally to the gender roles that are so difficult to change.

Work

Work is an important part of the lives of all the men in the group. The group provides an opportunity to describe our feelings about our relationships in work, both good and bad, as well as actual failures and successes. It has made us appreciate that we do have some good working relationships, and to enjoy that aspect of our work. But work isn't everything . . .

Work takes a lot out of me and I know that just makes other things harder.

For most of my life work has been a colossal imposition. For the whole of my working life I have either been poorly paid, or overworked – or both. I have been abused, exploited, insulted, intimidated, indoctrinated, violated, and little regard has been paid to my health, personal safety or general well-being. I get quite cross now when it is suggested that men have a good time of things at work. I can think of a thousand things that I would far rather be doing and in which I could find greater fulfilment.

Where I do find fulfilment, in my present job, it is mostly of the typically male kind, in organizing other people, for example, or winning over others in one way or another. Success here is measured in terms of status and approbation.

This is changing and I am finding another side to myself but it is almost impossible, I think, to put away that typically male behaviour because there is so much pressure for its continuation. I probably wouldn't even be able to do my job without it.

When I joined the group my self-image was very much based on my work. Since then I have learnt and grown in other areas of my life – leisure and family relationships – often due to insights and emotional strengths derived from the group.

The group is such a contrast to my relationships with men at work.

Relations between men

The culture in which we live leaves very little space for men to talk to each other on a personal level.

[My] previous experience of all-male groups has involved continual jostling for position and interpersonal point scoring: tea breaks at my last job were all about survival.

Men in the main are astonishingly bad at listening and giving each other support, presumably because it acknowledges weakness. I have tried many times before to open up to other men but the typical response is either embarrassment, or being told that I have to be tougher, or they start competing and telling you how bad *their* problems are. I was lying in hospital once after a serious car crash with crushed legs and chest injuries, etc., and a crowd of friends were round my bedside. One particularly domineering friend was standing unusually quietly at the foot of my bed for quite some time before suddenly piping up, 'You think that's bad, you ought to see my bollock.'

I am a straight male yet I am not at all put off by men. I wish we could all get as close to each other as women do without feeling threatened.

I am learning that dropping hints about emotional crises to a group of men is risky – much better to come right out with it – then the support is forthcoming.

Touching

A recurring theme in our self-questioning as a group is our theoretical avowal of greater freedom of physical contact between men, which contrasts with our rather limited expression of it.

Somewhere the group has got hold of the idea that improved closeness between men is measurable by the amount of touching, hugging, kissing that goes on, and there are spasmodic attempts to pay lip service to this idea or even more. I have in fact felt quite terrified by the whole thing, needing some help over the initial hurdles and even then wanting it very tokenized. But I do like to cross some of the hurdles in order to confirm my own suspicions about what my feelings, and those of various other members, might in fact be. I anticipate these feelings as being a complex layering of guilt, furtiveness, joyful liberation and infantile innocence, and probably a wish to reject so as to anticipate and offset rejection.

I have found it easier to spontaneously hug or to hold hands with a man. The accepted view seems to be that a straight man is unwilling to do this because of homophobia – however, as a straight man, I find it easier to be physically close to gay and bisexual men. I think it is because they are more relaxed about it than straight men, so maybe the whole thing is just a matter of practice. In any case, I have learnt that there is half a world out there whose physical closeness I have always ignored, and what a terrible waste this has been.

Talking and listening

When I thought about it the main group of people from which I wanted support and understanding was men.

As a men's group we seek to create our own forum for men's talk which does not exist in the wider social world, but which we are helping to establish.

The first time I went to the group and experienced talking openly among other men it was a real eye-opener. Everything felt so relaxed and uncompetitive. I love to hear men being so open with each other and listening so supportively.

Compassion – from men! Allowing myself to empathize with hurt, anger, hatred, cynicism, sadness, has been hard to do – threatening, I guess.

The main benefit of the group for me is that I can now talk to other men, both within the group and, more importantly, outside it, in a freer and more open way. It has enabled me to be more honest with myself, and with other men (and women). I have begun to value myself more, and to appreciate the feelings of others in a more understanding way. This has had a double effect. It has made me become more attractive to others and to myself.

Gender roles

We believe that men have a right to choose not to be condemned to the traditional male role.

I am incredibly envious of women in so many ways, so much so now that I actually feel cheated by the accident of my masculinity and by all of the agencies of the *status quo* that helped to drive me into that male mould.

I watch women a lot. I watch how much they smile compared with their scowling and grimacing male counterparts, I watch how they quite naturally touch or hold each other as they spontaneously express their feelings and how easily they can cry and then be comforted. I envy the way they can dress and look so stunning in ways that are just not open to most straight men, and certainly those of my generation. I love the way they can just open up about themselves and not be under any threat whatsoever for doing so. I cannot see any reason why I should be denied any of this just because I am a straight male. If only we could all get as close to each other as women do without feeling threatened.

I wish we could learn to be sensuous just like women but I think a lot of men who think like this are probably lost for want of a role model to slot into. I don't want to feel that I have to be gay or branded as weak or ineffectual or 'effeminate' (whatever that means) just in order to express the more sensitive and passive side of my sexuality.

I sometimes feel that we are still trapped in the dominant mode of male discourse, worried mainly about work rather than relationships, boastful or anxious about our unbridled sexuality rather than questioning its underlying assumptions, or assuming a heterosexuality, rather than a bisexuality or homosexuality. But at least we have begun to question ourselves.

Gender roles are not a safe subject for me unless carefully channelled with housework, marital responsibilities, etc. My boldest moment was recently when I dared, following the examples set by some gender-safe types I know, to say that I didn't give a shit about the World Cup, and felt glad at being able to say so without eyebrows being raised. When someone followed this later with a confession that he had been watching everything, there were remarks about the Group needing to have at least one 'real man' around. Very safe, in the context we have established together.

Housework is a recurring theme in our meetings, in which there always seems to be a conflict between a necessary division of labor and falling back on safe conventional gender roles.

Inevitably, our contributions to the maintenance of our home have become divided up, with me taking over responsibility for the more traditionally male aspects, such as maintaining the building, while she organizes the housework. Within this framework I do whatever housework I can. I need to preserve at least some sense of responsibility for housework and I would resent being solely responsible for jobs such as maintaining the car or insulating the loft were it not that she puts in so much elsewhere.

Do we feel and share responsibility, rather than just make the classic token gesture?

Having once been 'dispossessed' through divorce my little house means a great deal to me and keeping it in order helps me to maintain an identity with it. I really need this and I think I understand how women feel about their homes. Ironically, I now find that when the housework, or the responsibility for it, is being taken over by my partner I feel very threatened, as though my home is in danger of being taken away from me again.

MEN IN THE FAMILY

We find that thoughts and feelings about our families never fade from our sight. Our parents, our children, us as children, parents dying – so many of our strong feelings revolve around these relationships.

Parents

We have often talked about our relationships with our parents . . .

I suddenly realized how much I owed to my Mum and Dad and how I had never told them. I went straight home and wrote thanking them. This was shortly before my mum's death, and I'm so glad I was able to do it.

On one occasion I felt a strong need to talk about my anxieties in relating to women. I gradually, almost imperceptibly, got round to talking about my mum – a lot fell into place that evening.

I had lost my mother twice before she died. First going to school, surviving the home-sickness by denying the loss, and returning home to find nothing was the same. And then leaving home for real, and finding they were not the all-powerful, wise and supportive parents I had somehow assumed. They had become possessive and disapproving.

My relationship with my parents really means my relationship with my father. I love my mum dearly although superficially I appear not to be especially close to her and she sees much more of my sisters. My father, though, left me with enough hang-ups to last me several lifetimes. He was weak and deeply insecure and thus overpowering of those closest to him, especially the only other male in the household. The older I got, the more obsessive he seemed to be about keeping me in my place. The harder this became for him, the more he resorted to guilt games in order to get his way. 'You do what you like: it doesn't matter about me – I'm just the man of the house' are words that still ring in my ears even now that I am in my early forties and my father is dead. I have pretty well learned to live with this now but I know that I still have a deep-seated need for the approval that he gave so sparingly and grudgingly.

He was hurt that we had rejected all he had done for us, and wasted the money spent on our education. 'I could have bought a row of terraced houses with the money.' When I was small he was often unavailable: either away, in front of the TV news, or busy with his own friends. It is only as a father myself that I realize how little of a father he was to us. Much of the time with my son is spent doing the things my father never did with me. In trying to be a better father I am also reliving my childhood through my son.

Children

Children feature strongly in many discussions, and it has been a great relief to be able to acknowledge the extent that our children can make us feel good or bad.

The delight of being a father has been tempered with the feelings of guilt and inadequacy. More feelings that are difficult to express and not what is expected from fathers. To meet with a group of other men and fathers with different but not dissimilar feelings provides some reassurance to my efforts.

I am ashamed that I find little children so difficult because basically I like them so much. I always want to kiss and cuddle little babies – they're like a tit all over – but they require much patience. I even get really broody from time to time.

Hearing others relate their feelings and experiences with their own children has helped me to reflect on mine. I have to stop myself from urging my sons to join a men's group. Being in the group has helped me to be more aware of the issues between me and my teenage son.

My own two boys are in their early teens now and I couldn't begin to describe how much I love them. I feel much closer to them now than I did when they were younger, even though they no longer live with me. I hold them as much as I can – they clearly enjoy this and I hope they can always feel safe in physical contact with other males.

One of the most difficult issues that we have touched upon has been our attitudes to the sexuality of our daughters. Watching my daughter grow up is a great privilege. Being right there with them as their essential femaleness develops is a great privilege, but it can also be disturbing when their sexuality is apparent. I was very tentative in raising this issue, as it is almost asking for some coarse, insensitive comment – I was relieved by the understanding I got.

Childhood

Sessions where we discuss childhood disturb me. I have memories – lots of them – about my childhood. But the gaps in what I remember seem vaster still.

Reflecting on my feelings as a little boy makes me realize how little I understood them. My mother proposed a culture that said you should ignore your feelings and get on with life. From an early age I remember life as a struggle to be better. Better than before or better than someone else.

My childhood was a prolonged period of intense fantasy and I took an awfully long time to grow out of it. I probably still haven't entirely but I don't mind that any more. As an ado- lescent, of course, I was horrified by the vestiges of childhood ways but now I envy the candor of childhood and if I recognize anything remotely like that in myself I try not to fight it down. Being 'manly' and 'grown up' all the time seems a bit boring, actually.

To realize how much I enjoyed my teens – ah, the pleasures of mutual masturbation!

Growing up has been confusing and uncomfortable. I have made two attempts to 'get my head together' and work it all out. My first experience of therapy helped me feel better and understand myself a little. The strength of the Men's Group is that we have no ready answers. The process of sharing and trying to understand the confusions in our lives does more than explaining them. I still feel unhappy about my childhood and confused about my parents' deaths, but I don't feel that's so wrong or peculiar any more.

Bereavement

A number of us have suffered the recent death of a parent. A recurring theme is that of 'unfinished business' and the difficulties of redefining a relationship with a parent before their death.

My mother died earlier this year, and I never did finish my business with her. I had acknowledged the impossibility of this a long time before and her death did not bring the anguish that I had expected – in fact I had started mourning her about two years previously. And now I feel I have discovered a new friend in my father, and look forward to all our future time together.

When my mother died unexpectedly, grief did not get a look in. I was finally free of the possessive force trying to make me part of a 'family' I no longer believed in, and I was now going to be subjected to the family grieving again. I was surprised that when it was all over, I still did not feel much loss. I must have lost her too many times before. Widowed, my father sank into an alcoholic depression that within ten years resulted in a fatal heart attack. I can't say I did much to help. His crises were dealt with by my elder brother, with little gratitude from my father. He remained belligerent and unsupportive to me. In spite of some minor reconciliation in the last few months of his life, his death seemed more inconvenient than sad. My son will miss him, but I am still cross that he was no more of a grandfather to him than he was a father to me.

MEN AS PARTNERS

Our relationships to a wife, partner, or current lover are the focus of much of our discussion. We watch each other trying to deal with the daily negotiations, pleasures and frustration; in the long time our group has been together, we have shared in the excitement of new relationships, the pleasure of discovery, and the later struggle and uncertainty. Lots of laughs, and some tears. For many of us this is the 'frontline' when it comes to trying to change as men.

Men can be born, grow up, be lovers, husbands, fathers, and yet still never reach out and just be with the people around them. Being in the group, realizing I could genuinely love my daughter, and separating from my wife all added to make me realize that I had been going around in a bubble all my life. I got a determination that I would open myself to those around me, and in particular would allow myself the joy of just being with my partner, instead of incessantly planning and doing. As someone said at a weekend men's gathering I went to, 'I want to be a human being, not a human doing.' But I found this was not easy to keep up – there seems to be a natural inertia that pulls me back to within myself, afraid of failing, and unable to share the fears. Fortunately my partner is prepared to help me by pointing out when I am 'away' from her in my thoughts and feelings, even though I am physically close.

Sex

Sex is a difficult issue to talk about in the group . . . . The group has been the first situation in which I have heard problems about sex being openly, if very tentatively, discussed among men.

But . . .

Not wanting to betray my partner's privacy – not quite trusting the group to be kind enough.

Talking about sex has helped some of us to deal more effectively with ourselves as well as with relationships.

Acknowledgement of masturbation, and the pleasure and relaxation of sleeping on one's own, have also featured, and have been related to being able to admit to the tension that sex can introduce to a long-running relationship. We have also managed to introduce a lot of humour into this discussion, and so gone some way to counter the envy I have always felt towards (how I imagine) women can discuss sex.

I really do enjoy my body, it fascinates me and I fully intend to experience as much bodily pleasure as I possibly can for as long as I can. I think that my feelings about it make it much easier for me to empathize with my partner. She also fascinates me and I try to give her the sort of pleasure that I love to receive myself.

Beginning to talk more openly about sex has helped us to deal with unresolved guilt and self-consciousness about it:

Gradually I have started to be able to see my sexuality as something not to hide, not to be embarrassed by, not to confine between the sheets in the dark.

I gained a new-found optimism, honesty and openness. I discovered a greater confidence in myself in relation to my sexual partner.

I look forward to a more thorough-going analysis of the whole business of sex, if only to reveal something of the very great variety which I think is its real characteristic.

Monogamy

Ultimately, we are all searching for relationships which are as satisfying as we can achieve.

All types of relationship are represented in the group, and a lot of dissatisfaction with arrangements have been expressed. The main lesson I have learnt is the absurdity of expecting a single individual to provide all the varied aspects of support and care that we each need – it is neither fair on the recipient nor the giver. Many people can be important, and in many ways. How much this acknowledgement of the importance of others should extend into sexual relations is something on which we have never been able to come to any conclusion, and it seems to remain for each individual to settle with their partner.

It has felt like a privilege to be in the regular company of people enjoying such varied models of partnership. At times I have felt very unambitious to be married – but increasingly my efforts within marriage have felt worthwhile and right for me.

I know a lot of people, mostly male, who think that monogamy is not in our nature. That may well be the case but we don't live in a state of nature, we live in a world with a culture and a code of morals, and a promise to be monogamous is important, precisely because it is a promise, usually a very important one to the other person. That is the issue for me, not whether monogamy is right or wrong, natural or otherwise.

Coming out

For a long time we skirted around the possibility of sexual desire towards other men, making vague liberal references to an inherent bisexuality.

I felt it was too threatening to the social relationship between the men in the group to admit to my sexual desire for other men.

That changed when one man openly described himself as bisexual, with a friendly throwing down of the gauntlet – 'That's me, folks' – which others felt at first to be quite shattering but which inspired more sudden and gradual revelations. The resultant change of balance between 'straight' and 'gay' opened up a wider range of discussion on sexual-bodily issues, which some found actually shifted and helped them reassess their own sexuality.

Getting to know other gay men has been a terrific learning experience for me, and a humbling one too. Sharing my awkwardness about my sexuality has been a relief.

One of the greatest benefits I have obtained from the group is the chance to change my attitude to gay and bisexual men, simply by being friends and sharing experiences. It has made me carefully examine my own sexuality, and realize the limitations I have lived under. Although I have stayed straight, I now see classic heterosexual penetrative sex as being just a single, rather restricted expression of my sexuality. I have realized that I have so much to learn, and probably more about receiving than giving.

Coming out was one of the most important turning points for me in the group. It felt a tremendous relief for me to relate socially to other bisexual men. I felt so isolated before.

MEN AS THEMSELVES

The group has settled on personal development as a primary aim. Yet surprisingly little time is devoted to strictly personal issues; we find it easier to address the task indirectly by considering our places in society and the family. But over a number of years we have occasionally discussed these topics more explicitly.

Our bodies

Becoming aware of our bodies in a shared and conscious way is one area of discussion which enabled me to overcome the shame I felt about my own body and to appreciate its vibrancy and beauty with other men. Talking about my body hair, penis size, fat, shape and other taboo areas of male guilt and shame allowed me to appreciate the male body in a way I had previously withheld.

We once had a mildly structured session in which we outlined what we did and didn't like about our bodies, which I found challenging and self-revealing, and reassuring in its non-sexual atmosphere. In another discussion, about body hair, a member went to check up on his chest hair, but turned away to the window to do it. I wouldn't have, I think, and I count this as something of an advance.

My body is an enormous source of pleasure to me and I have very little sense of shame about it. I am quite comfortable walking around the house naked and I have no guilt whatsoever about masturbation.

When I am being cuddled I often feel very little and very safe and I couldn't give a hoot what anyone has to say about it.

We talked about clothes one time. I went out and had my hair professionally cut and styled for the first time in years.

I have never been able to admit, either to myself or others, that I was not feeling physically good. By hearing men describe how they were feeling physically, and the extremely close connection to their general state of mind, I have realized how liberating it can be to admit to feeling bad. By being nicer to ourselves, we do not necessarily enter into a lifetime of idle self-indulgence.

Emotions

For men there are 'safe' emotions such as anger and laughter and 'unsafe' emotions, such as crying, which seem only to be allowed under the most extreme circumstances. I hardly ever cry. When I reached puberty I used to have to fight tears down. After a while, though, they just didn't come any more.

When men are moved to tears or any other sensitive state, they seem to idealize it. In songs or on the big screen or on the football pitch, a man in tears can achieve almost heroic status. My father, though, couldn't watch a man cry on the television at all; he would get angry and leave the room.

After a close friend of mine dropped dead without warning I found myself trying to make sense of the whole business of men crying. Of course, I had no idea just how much I loved him while he was alive, and after he died I found myself dissolving into tears at anything that reminded me of him. It provided such a sense of relief to be able to deal with my grief in this way that I eventually began to wonder why I couldn't unburden myself in this way in the normal course of events when feeling upset. In time, though, this passed and although I still cannot just shed tears whenever I ought to, I can feel that they are much closer to the surface now. It feels much better like that.

I still feel imprisoned in the 'boys don't cry' attitudes of my early upbringing, though I know all about the more liberated attitudes I claim to be subscribing to.

When one of us has been very low, in a way that as an individual I would have found very difficult to deal with, I have learnt that as a group we have resources for caring. Similarly, we are good at sharing joy and laughter. Anger we find more difficult.

The emotion I like least is myself in my anger. This can explode like a geyser and alarms those who are closest to me. I can see my father's anger in my anger, but also my anger at him for all of his oppressive and humiliating ways. It comes mostly when I feel cornered with no line of escape. If I can just get away briefly and calm down I know I can deal with it but often that is not possible.

MEN AND FEMINISM

Whatever happened to the politics? We set out with the aim of campaigning openly against sexism – this has never really materialized.

Sometimes I regret that we do not do more active campaigning, but I don't have much time for that at the moment and I think there are other important issues if I did.

We are not a 'feminist' group.

As a group we still have a problem in that it sometimes feels that the form of talk that we establish goes no further than the group and the immediate social world. The talk remains private, confidential and closeted. Its impact on the wider world is not obvious. The change that occurs is only personal, piecemeal and fragmented.

We started as a self-help group and sexism has been a recurring theme because it is around us all the time, in our relationships and at work.

What on earth would a woman make of all this?

I realize that all this, to a feminist, will sound like a group of men being nice to each other in order to make up for the emotional poverty of their lives, and that there is no mention of the structure of power in our society that places men in control. What does our group do in acknowledging this, and what do we actively do about changing it? Perhaps very little.

For all our right-on-ness and conscientious desire to be enlightened and non-sexist we are still a group of men bringing with us the legacy of our male mentors, upbringing and experiences. Are we just playing the same old power-hungry male games in a fashionably enlightened disguise? Can we expect to make any real progress without more dialogue with women?

SUMMARY

From its initial impetus as a response to women's conscious-ness-raising groups and the Women's Movement, our group has slowly evolved towards a group which takes and makes its own bearings. No longer about envy or emulation of women's groups, although still 'fellow travellers,' we are attempting to create our own discourse.

We are in no way 'model men,' but at least we have begun to question ourselves and to be less frightened of our feelings. Through our group we have found for ourselves that men do have the capacity for self-criticism, and can be open to change. It may seem rather a cliché to say that we want to be in touch with our emotions, and break free from the male stereotype, but these are not easy tasks and the onus is on us to keep working and try to change.

We want to be able to be proud to be men.

Chapter 8

A gay man's reflections on the men's movement

Martin Humphries

This essay concerns my experience as a member of the Achilles Heel Collective from 1978 to 1982, the expression of hatred towards gay men, and relations between gay and non-gay men today. The reason I wish to go back into the past is to give you some sense of the direction of my politics before you read my opinions about how I see the world and what can be done to improve it. What, you may ask, has this to do with 'men and feminism?' The simple answer, which is explored in greater detail below, is that until we recognize the spectrum of sexual difference as horizontal rather than vertical, men are unlikely to change in the ways that feminism, rightly, demands that we do. As a gay man I am personally committed to change; as a pro-feminist gay male socialist I am personally and politically committed to improving the world we all live in. Actions can speak louder than words, but words can be a stimulant towards action, and I hope that if I explain some of my own history you will be able to understand my perspective and be encouraged to believe that change is possible.

THE POLITICS OF ACHILLES HEEL

In 1979, I was coming out more strongly as a gay man, recovering from the breakdown of a monogamous relationship and looking for political involvement. Straight Left groups I found alienating because of their negative attitudes towards lesbians and gay men. I wasn't aware of any gay socialist groups. I was (am) white, middle-class with some knowledge of feminist theory and little knowledge of socialist theory. I felt inarticulate and wanted to find a group with whom to work and learn. I had recently started going to a gay consciousness-raising group which, though challenging and supportive, wasn't all that I wanted. It was at this moment that I read *Achilles Heel No. 1*. I was excited to read material by a group of men who acknowledged the importance of feminist and gay politics in their lives and wanted to find out more about them.

Achilles Heel is a pro-feminist, anti-sexist writing and publishing collective committed to supporting men writing about sexual politics and socialism. Most of the work appeared in a journal of the same name which was first published in 1978. I joined the collective in December 1978 with a hazy idea that a way forward was through building and establishing political alliances with non-gay men who were committed to sexual politics. In this context I was a gay man working with pro-feminist men – some of whom had relationships with men but did not clearly define themselves as gay – to produce a journal of anti-sexist (men's) politics. At that time I was politically untutored; how 'tutored' I am now is open to debate. I had a personal awareness of the oppression of gay men and felt that feminism aligned with socialism offered a concrete way of changing the world. My political his-story, in terms of learning and understanding theory, was only just beginning. I was searching for ways to develop.

I went, somewhat nervously, to my first editorial meeting. Initially my relationship was rather peripheral. I listened to some discussion and organized when and how material would be proofread. I liked the men I met – there was warm camaraderie between them, yet they were, unlike other non-gay men I knew, articulate in expressing doubt and uncertainty and willing to talk openly about their inner emotional worlds. This is not to say that meetings were not difficult – they were often stormy and argumentative – but underneath there was a cohesive sense of purpose.

I'm sure that my being gay was one of the reasons they asked me to join – political credibility can be a motivating force – but it was not the only reason: I also had a perspective that they did not. I knew that I was gay from an early age and grew up hiding parts of myself, experiencing a process of subterfuge in a particularly focused way. Such an experience can have many debilitating effects, but it does enable you intuitively to recognize the distortions of the world. Later, when I read or heard theories of sexual politics, I recognized within it elements from my own life. For the other men in the collective it was different. While they had strong emotional and sometimes sexual relationships with men, they saw their relationships with feminist women as primary. Often their experience and understanding of sexual politics was developed through their interaction with socialist/feminist women or through their friends in the gay movement.

In some ways we were a unified group. We were all in men's groups, and we all held a basic commitment to exploring the challenges of feminist, gay, and socialist politics, while actively creating and working out a real anti-sexist way of living. We were all interested in building supportive relationships with men, and in exposing the absurdities of traditional masculinity. But in other ways we were a diverse group that experienced the pains and frustrations of collective working. Differences would appear sharply. Many were the contradictions, but rich was the hope that we could find ways of exploring or resolving them. Ways that would enable, support and encourage other men to find, or begin to find, patterns of living that were not oppressive to women and other men. High-flown ideals. Too ambitious, maybe, but we attempted it and in the process created openings that had not been seen by many men before.

Towards the summer of 1979 Ian joined the collective; now we were eight. Both Pauls were involved with child-care. Andy and Steve were single-parent fathers. James and Vic lived in mixed houses. Ian lived in a squat and I shared a hard-to-let flat with another gay man. All of us were involved in radical politics. Some of us were into therapy. All went to the cinema, ate, slept, made love, had sex, and attempted to work out our politics.

I was primarily involved in editorial discussion and production. We would meet fortnightly, increasing to weekly once production deadlines became clear. Much of the discussion was around the collective's relationship with and towards the feminist and gay movements. Although this discussion was reflected rather diffusely in our second issue, a lot of taking stock actually took place during this period. To some extent I was seen as an 'expert' on the gay movement, its current feelings and developments. I was uneasy about this and tried to discourage it by relating my personal experiences rather than generalizing. Within situations where I felt supported I did initiate or get involved in discussions of homophobia and gayness. Often it was hard, especially when I questioned their own heterosexuality. Some of these men had an intellectual commitment to gayness while others were interested in exploring the gayness within themselves.

One strongly felt difference was that I had a profound understanding of the oppression of patriarchy based on lived experience, while for them it was a reality more deeply buried. They were more concerned with learning to give up power, to break through a deadening masculinity. But perhaps this polarizes it too sharply, for I too am a man who had to learn (and still is learning) how to combat the wiles of patriarchy, particularly in situations with women. I had to learn to see my own sexism. My position was one of being politically united with feminism, experiencing some of the oppressions suffered by women while having some of the power of being a man. For the straight men in the group, a desire to change developed from unhappiness with the traditional roles of masculinity and the demands of feminist women. Sharing the experiences of our lives was a part of learning to see the political connections between our personal lives and the wider social sphere.

Meetings tended to be affectionate even though they were often heated. We would show up around 7:30 pm, welcome each other, often with an embrace, and talk until everyone had arrived. We would usually begin by reading and talking about letters received or other matters relating to the last issue, then we would draw up an agenda of things to discuss. This discussion would usually be about articles in progress or received, the questions they raised, or the next issue's editorial or theme. We tended to focus on the questions and how they related to us personally while attempting to ensure some level of theoretical debate. Meetings ended in embraces, and often in a trip to the pub.

The collective continued to grow; now we were twelve. Other men joined in much the same way as I had. This affected power relationships and tended to equalize them. When I first joined I was a newcomer among a group of men with a shared sense of history; by the fourth issue, I was one of the older members and my sense of newness had long since gone. Although we tried to avoid splitting into factions, we did tend to coalesce around particular issues. Those of us who felt strongly would unite. This happened most obviously in discussions of articles.

There was usually at least one contentious article submitted for each issue. If several of us didn't like the article we would form a group against those who wanted the article included and vice versa. We would attempt to work with the writer of the piece on the difficult areas until a majority of the collective felt able to agree to publication. Such differences were painful, particularly if the writer was a member of the collective.

Issue 4 was the first time another openly gay man was involved in the production of an issue. He was a man I knew through a gay affinity group who wrote an article about his experience of working in a factory. It was good for the collective to experience working with another gay man and it lifted the pressure from me. His being there gave me strength. During this time my own writing was encouraged and I went from being involved only in editorial discussions to writing poems and later articles for the special issues on violence and sexuality. The writing process was often hard for contributors as articles typically had to go through a number of drafts: nothing was printed unless a majority of the collective supported its inclusion. This meant that we each, at one time or another, had to cope with our own resentment of criticism. It was in this that our experience of being in men's groups was invaluable, for the way we discussed contributions, whether our own or from outside the collective, focused on wanting to draw out and construct rather than critically demolish.

For the special issue on male violence, we established a separate men's group within the collective so that we could work on the problem among ourselves. These meetings alternated with production meetings so progress on the issue was slow. Over a period of six months we met fortnightly to share our own experiences of violence or of being violent. Some of these meetings were taped and appeared in the issue in the editorial and in an article based on the transcripts. It was an important process: how could we as men publish an issue on male violence without having explored all the issues on a personal/political level ourselves? This way of working was, for me, one of the most exciting things about being involved in this group of non-gay men.

Something very complex was the issue of sexual desire between men in the collective. There is a commonly held view that the relationship of gay and non-gay men is always one in which we (the gay men) are in the subordinated/desiring role and they (the heterosexual men) are in the superior/admired one. I did not wish to uphold this theory, desiring, in practice, to have a sexual relationship with another 'out' gay man. It was not a problem until Ian joined the collective to work on issue 3. Up to that point I had experienced pleasure in being affectionate with these men and had occasional masturbation fantasies about them, but felt that we were a band of brothers; with Ian it was different. I became infatuated with him. He was very confusing. I felt shy of him yet he obviously liked me, liked being with me, liked giving me a hug. But I felt unable to push it any further without any clear signals from him. I felt stupid spending so much time thinking about him; it was like being back at school! Would he be at the next meeting? Could I sit next to him? If the meeting was in the East End would he give me a lift home? If the meeting was at my place would he stay behind? Would we make love? etc. etc. He did stay behind after one meeting and we did talk about love – not mine for him – then, after a long silence, he left. I wrote poems about him but never gave them to him. I felt angry with myself. It was so completely fruitless. I knew that he was a love-object but that didn't remove the desire.

In direct contrast, when Chris joined the collective a year later there was an immediate affinity between us. He knew gay men, was close to a gay man in his men's group and was open to exploring his own feelings. We would see each other outside of meetings and developed a closeness which has changed but not been lost over the years. I desired him and he had feelings of desire for me. We flirted a lot and were regarded, for a while, as lovers (or nearly so) by the rest of the collective. We were always together in meetings, often arriving or leaving together, we touched a lot and talked easily. There was sharing between us. We first slept together when we went to Bristol for the 1980 anti-sexist men's conference. In Chris's own words we 'melted.' Sleeping together was delightful; sex was more problematic. Chris didn't wish to experiment with me, yet his sexual experience with men was so limited that sex between us couldn't be anything but experimentation. He wanted to experience pleasure, give me pleasure, express his feelings physically, but did that mean he was gay? It was both safe, in that he knew me, and dangerous, in that sex with me brought up questions for him about his own sexuality that he didn't want to answer. After Bristol it became clear to both of us that the sex didn't work. I didn't mind, at least we had both taken the risk. Unlike my experience with Ian, our relationship was much more mutual, one in which we established boundaries together.

I was also aware, at times, of reciprocal feelings of desire among other members of the collective. When we were working well together an element of sexual desire was expressed in our physical behavior; we touched each other more. I do not know if there is such a thing as 'radical' male bonding, or if in some way all groupings of men are oppressive by their very nature, but I do know that it is possible within our lives to create relationships which are of such depth that we can continue to struggle and survive.

Despite political differences, changing awareness and power shifts within the collective, we were a support group to each other. We had a structure within which we could challenge, ask without fear and explore the difficulties of living. This meant that we brought our experiences of various external pressures into the collective discussion. One of these pressures for me was criticism from other gays for working with non-gay men – though they were not called that by my critics. The question would be: *Why was I putting my energies into Achilles Heel when our own struggles needed support?* I would respond to this in two ways. One was defensive in that I pointed out that Achilles Heel was not my only political activity and went on to describe the other work I did with lesbians and gay men. If I felt stronger I would argue about the importance of establishing relationships with non-gay men who supported the gay movement. Over the years my feelings about working with non-gay men have changed. Initially my involvement was not thought out; since then I have come to recognize more deeply the political importance of gay and non-gay men working together.

In some areas of my life, I would rather work with the men of Achilles Heel – or men like them – than with some of my gay brothers with whom I have no connection other than a liking for sex with men. I have more in common – in terms of how I live, how I want to live, how I work, how I want the future to be – with some anti-sexist men than I do with gay men whose lifestyle is based on consumerism. This is not to deny the validity of gay socialists working autonomously. Without first working separately and discovering our strengths, it is not possible to conceive of working together. Although self-labeling can give us strength, it can also constrict. Saying that you are gay is a political act, but it doesn't define your politics. I'm a socialist and my dreams of how I would like the world to be are shaped by this. It's a dream I feel I share with some, though not all, gay men.

STILL FIGHTING AFTER ALL THESE YEARS

Heterosexuality is the love that need not speak its name. Only homosexuals are ever likely to refer to it by its full one; the complacent hetero thinks of it as sexuality entire. Who but the homosexual ever thinks to mention that Torquemada, Attila the Hun, Genghis Khan, Hitler, Mussolini, Stalin and Jack the Ripper were all heterosexuals (and men). Who ever says that the vast majority of child molesters, child abusers and rapists are heterosexual men, or that the pornography which most damages women is heterosexual. Those of us to whom heterosexuals are 'they' clearly see a different world. Though we may inhabit the same social spaces, we often see and experience them so differently that we remain at least one world apart.[1]

Homophobia is a fancy word that means fear and hatred of homosexuals. I will devote this second part of my essay to the issue as one that I can speak of from my own experience, that is essential for non-gay men to continue to grapple with, and that plays a key role in the current backlash against gay people that we see, for example, in the media representation of AIDS, the Church of England witch-hunt and Section 28 of the 1988 Local Government Act in Britain.

Section 28 makes it illegal for local government monies to be spent on anything that can be considered the 'promotion' of homosexuality. (A group called AARGH – Artists Against Rampant Government Homophobia – has produced a comic book mercilessly exposing the absurdities and the realities of the law.) The Act of which it is a part was introduced by the Conservative Government to exert greater control over the activities of Metropolitan and County Councils; targeting lesbians and gay men in Section 28 was an easy way to ensure that the Act would achieve the necessary support. The Section is a blatant attempt to strip us of the means to educate, communicate, and organize, to stifle our voices and drive us back into the closet. The result is that the funding of many lesbian and gay groups by local councils has stopped, the media have had a field day of gay-bashing, and yet more young people are taught in the schools that being lesbian or gay is awful, disgusting, depraved.

The one good thing about Section 28 is that the response against it has been overwhelming. Lesbians and gay men have been working together politically to prove yet again that lesbian and gay rights are human rights, and this time support from heterosexuals has been encouraging. Section 28 is only the latest in a series of explicit attacks which began with the media barrage against gay men as a result of the onset of AIDS. We have become used to being tagged as twilight men who live sleazy lives and to the exposés of the famous who happen to be 'So.'[2] But AIDS unleashed the most vitriolic, homophobic press reporting my generation has seen. Gay men have been presented as inherently evil and responsible for the deaths of innocents. We are the devil's spawn who rejoice in spreading contagion, the scapegoats for society's most pernicious ills. Not surprisingly, the incidence of attacks – sometimes fatal – on gay men has increased. I wrote this poem in 1985 to give voice to my anger.

PERFORMANCE WITHOUT A PRODUCTION[3]

Not our disease
A hard fact to realise
Like 1 in 8,000 are positive
   19,712 since 1982
   2742 dead
    78% gay[4]
And rising.

More die on the roads each year.
Cancer kills. How many?
Mortality is not quantifiable.
Ah, but, they say, isn't
AIDS a form of suicide
The Lemming factor
Collective death wish
Wrath of god on the 'unnatural'
OUR FAULT
Say christian churches
  mothers union
  the new right

Bernard Manning
Donna Summer
Anita Bryant
Ian Paisley
Louie 'shoot the queers' Welch[5]
Keith Hays[6] who put an ad in the New Zealand newspapers
which said:
'Stop the killer disease AIDS
The homosexual lifestyle is a death style.'

In return we spit on them.[7]

A good story Death
makes headlines
put it with gay and circulation guaranteed.
The press have it every which way.

Fear, like soap opera, is addictive
spreads like the plague
in us too
as we suffer.

'Being defined by our cocks
is literally killing us' says Ned Weeks.[8]
What's defined is homosexuality
It has nothing to do with being gay.

In 1889 homosexuality was a dis-ease
incurable they found it,
don't know how it spreads
– one born every minute –

In 1969 we came out
to hit consumerism.
Consume or die,
consume and die.

Exposing ourselves we danced
stretching boundaries we danced
changing our arms we danced
changing the world we danced.
Danced on the rim of the world.

Now dirge enters disco
carried in by us
we're told. Huh!

So, we change the music
'the body is a site of pleasure'[9]
we shift the pleasures sited
and learn in layer upon layer
of experience built up over time.

We know or will know people who've died
Amongst the causes of death is AIDS
I may have AIDS – who knows?
If I do, it is
not the 'natural' consequence of being gay,
not my disease begot by me.
It is an illness.
An invasion of the body, my body, our bodies.

No different from the way
their world
invades and proscribes ours.

A fear of the 'other' exists in all of us. When gays are beaten up it is usually by men who are scared of their own gay feelings. This fear is homophobia, and we see it everywhere, from the casual justification of the murder of a gay man to the bumper sticker advising drivers, 'Help Stamp Out AIDS: Run Over a Queer.'

Every time I see a report of the suicide of a young woman or man I wonder, as many lesbians and gay men wonder, if that was yet another gay kid who couldn't take it any more. What is it that we can't take? From the moment we are born we learn that lesbians and gay men are not acceptable, that we are perverts, queers, nancy boys, poofters, brown hatters, bumboys and now AIDS carriers, so that we are not only the unacceptable face of masculinity but also the harbingers of death. Culturally gay men experience death all the time. We are constantly told that we don't exist. We grow up as though we don't exist. We all have to come out. 'I thought I was the only one' – don't we all experience this? Some gay men never recover from their upbringing. How many gay men do you know who've committed suicide?

Boys are taught to be boys, boys are taught to be men – we all know that, have some understanding of the way it happens, how the fabric of patriarchal society is organized around the development of the MAN. We all live with the fact that we do not match the stereotype, we spend the rest of our lives adjusting, coming to terms with, accepting what we really are. Learning to love ourselves so that we can be ourselves. Learning to resist. Learning to acknowledge the fears and go on from there. I was part of a fortunate generation – although I never would have known this when I was bullied at school for being a sissy – in that I became involved in the gay movement in my early twenties. Through this experience and through feminism I was able to be positive about my sexuality and develop a friendship network that supports, challenges, and protects me. This is not true for many of us, as this extract from a poem by Jim Everhard, who died of AIDS in 1989, makes clear.

CURING HOMOSEXUALITY[10]

for three incurables, Frank, Stu and Richard

'There are no homosexuals, only fallen heterosexuals.'
(*Dr Reuben Sebastian Wildchild*)

Of the many known and proven
cures for homosexuality,
the most familiar, perhaps,
is the Catholic Church's version of
'Confession-is-good-for-the-soul.'

According to this ritual, every time
you feel an unclean urge to touch yourself, you stop your hand with the
mental image of the Pope staring you
in the face and these words: 'If-I-do-this-
I-have-to-tell-the-priest-again.'
Then, when you go to confession you
enumerate and fully describe every such
forbidden act leaving out not the
slightest detail and the priest,
who lives anonymously in a dark box,
tells you what you must do to redeem your lost
soul . . .

      . . . If this doesn't work,
and one wonders about these
good men whose career it is to sit in the dark
and listen to the pornography of everybody
else's life, the next step is psychoanalysis.

The doctor sits solemnly in the dark
behind you, his hands suspiciously folded
in his lap, and doesn't say a word
while you lie down on a long lumpy sofa
and tell him about your childhood
and how much you hate yourself
for thinking the things you think
so uncontrollably
and you wish your tongue would fall out
and it almost does as you go on and on
wondering what the hell this fellow
is listening for as you start inventing
stories about Uncle's anus and house pets.
You soon find out he is interpreting
the things you tell him. According to
psychoanalytic theory, everything you say
means something else even more sinister
than what you meant. Your unknown desires
live within you and control your outward behaviour. For instance, if you say . . .

. . . you had a dream about flying
he'll interpret it as a dream of sexual
frustration and penis envy meaning
you are really sick since only women
are supposed to have penis envy. He'll
probably ask you, 'How did you feel when
you first saw your father's instrument?
Did you notice if it was bigger than yours?
Did he seem ashamed of his? Did you want to touch it?'
If you tell him you don't recall
what it looked like he'll tell you
you unconsciously wanted it to fall off
so you could flush it down the toilet . . .

. . . If you tell him
you've had it, you're tired of wasting
time and money when you haven't even begun
talking about homosexuality, he'll tell you
your problems run even deeper than he
initially realized and you need hospitalization.

Once you are hospitalized, the doctors
will begin electric shock therapy.
They call it therapy. There is no resistance.
You are not sure who's getting the therapy,
you or the sadistic maniacs who strap you down
and wire you up and turn on the juice
while they flash pictures of naked men
on a screen. The idea is to associate pain
and the fear of death by electrocution
with naked men . . .

   . . . If
none of these cures works
you will probably be thrown out of high school
as a bad influence for all those guys who
make you suck them off in the shower,
then beat you up at the bus stop. If you
still wish to remain homosexual, you will probably be arrested in the public library
for browsing too long in the 'Sexuality'
section or during one of the periodic raids
of a local gay bar or face charges for soliciting
a cop who arrested you and forced you
to give him a blow job while he played
with his siren. In prison
you will probably be gang-raped by
lusty straight men who are only acting out
their healthy but stifled heterosexual impulses . . .

   . . . Once you are released
you will become an expert in American
legal procedures as you face future charges
of child molestation, murder and attempts
to overthrow the common decency, whatever that is.
When you have had it, and decide to hijack
a jet and escape, you will discover the small
but important fact that no nation under god
or red offers asylum, political or otherwise,
to a plane full of pansies . . .

   . . . In conclusion, there are no known cures
for homosexuality. Faggots have survived

Christianity, psychiatry, social ostracism, jail,
earth, air, wind and fire, as well as the pink
triangle and concentration camps. Nothing
can reckon with you if you can reckon with yourself.
The facts have been available for a long time:
where there are human beings, there are faggots.
We were around clubbing each other over the head
just like straight cave men. We were considered magical
by some people. We were considered mysterious.
We were obviously different but not always hated.
Hatred is always self-hatred.
Denial is always fear.
It's easier for THEM when
we hate ourselves,
FEAR OURSELVES.
I don't have to and
I WON'T.
None of us knows how he got here,
for what reason we are here or
why we are who we are.
It is not obvious
and a swish doesn't make it any more obvious
than the lack of one.
I am obvious
because I AM.

Being as we are can lead to receiving the most obvious form of homophobia – the physical attack (it can also lead to being able to survive the experience which is much more difficult if you're in the closet). Since school I have not (yet) been physically abused for being gay, I have been shouted at in the street and had men bump into me and say something unintelligible in an aggressive manner but blood has not been drawn, bruises raised or death resulted. Not true for friends who have been beaten and, in one instance, murdered – countless times I've read of the stabbings, beatings and murders of lesbians and gay men for no reason it would appear other than we breathe the same air.

For *Achilles Heel No. 5* I wrote an article on homophobia. At that time, 1981, I wore a gay badge most of the time. Even though now I rarely wear a gay badge except in demonstrations, much of what I said then is as relevant now.

Whenever I'm on the streets, in a pub, a park, a cottage or a shop, I'm aware of who is around me and how they're reacting to me. If it is during the evening or on the street I'm aware of who is in front, is someone behind, why are they walking fast, what are those men doing on the other side of the road? I try to keep alert and not fall into daydreams, to be prepared in case I'm about to be attacked physically or verbally. This may sound like paranoia (try wearing a gay badge and then see if it's our paranoia or yours) but such safety precautions are necessary as the incidence of attacks on gay men makes clear.

This is not a new experience for gay men, we have always been attacked (like women and people of colour). I knew this from a very early age. My life at school was a balancing act between not letting it be known I was gay for fear of the consequences and still being open to myself as much as possible – this involved delicate lying, it became an art as I failed to reveal the gender of those I had relationships with or fantasies about, and I also enjoyed the ambiguity. By the time I was 15 I led two lives: at school trying to be straight despite being bullied by those who saw me as a sissy and were upset by it; outside school spending hours cruising cottages looking for and spending time with men like myself. This involved a large amount of self-deception and went on until I was 17 and met an older man who showed me other aspects of the gay scene – though I didn't and haven't stopped cottaging – and from whom I realised it was possible to be openly gay with other people but only a small minority. He lost his job as a social worker after his boss discovered he was gay. I knew the barrier erected by straight society to prevent them knowing about gays was maintained by threats of physical violence and it took me several years before I rejected and challenged this threat and came out. Then and only then did I discover that the dangers of being out are more concrete and easier to deal with than those of remaining in the closet. Rather than the threats being intangible and heightened by silence they can be faced with a self-confidence previously unknown. This is not to say that all is easy, especially as attacks on gay people are increasing . . .

And what is it that these people are so fearful of? What are our workmates and families frightened of? What they are so frightened of is me and my friends and comrades and lovers.

What is so frightening about two men or many men loving each other or two women or many women loving each other? What is so frightening is that they know we have a distinctly gay identity and culture that goes far beyond sexual/emotional activity.[11] It is extremely old and it is continuous. We experience and see the world differently. As I explained earlier, this is partly brought about by the experience of growing up knowing that we are not the kind of woman or man everything around us tells us we should be. It was only when I was in my teens that I learnt some of the history of homosexuality and realised that forms of homosexual subcultures have existed since the beginning of time. This should be valued and treasured as it has been amongst other cultures in the past (American Indians for one). But it would appear to be too much to expect. Well, we all know something of the realities of male upbringing and how hard it is for men – including me – to relinquish the power that we are taught is a man's 'natural' right. Nature too is coerced into providing them with a reason to destroy us. The fact that heterosexual men are trapped by nature is, it would seem, of little account to most men – perhaps when that silence is broken things will really change and we will see, as Jon Ward says, alongside the welcoming of lesbian and gay culture a representation of male–female intercourse as a freely chosen option, claiming no privilege among erotic games because its relation to biological function has been transformed from one of *determination* to one of *coincidence*.[12]

So the world needs turning upside down, the silence needs to be broken, the fears confronted. How? Susan Griffin has a suggestion.

AN ANSWER TO A MAN'S QUESTION, 'WHAT CAN I DO ABOUT WOMEN'S LIBERATION?'[13]

Wear a dress.
Wear a dress that you made yourself, or bought in a dress store.
Wear a dress and underneath the dress wear elastic, around your hips, and underneath your nipples.
Wear a dress and underneath the dress wear a sanitary napkin.
Wear a dress and wear sling-back, high-heeled shoes.

Wear a dress, with elastic and a sanitary napkin underneath, and sling-back shoes on your feet, and walk down Telegraph Avenue.
Wear a dress, with elastic and a sanitary napkin and sling-back shoes on Telegraph Avenue and try to run.

Find a man.
Find a nice man who you would like to ask you for a date.
Find a nice man who *will* ask you for a date.
Keep your dress on.
Ask the nice man who asks you for a date to come to dinner.
Cook the nice man a nice dinner so the dinner is ready before he comes and your dress is nice and clean and wear a smile.
Tell the nice man you're a virgin, or don't have
birth control, or you would like to get to know him better.
Keep your dress on.
Go to the movies by yourself.

Find a job.
Iron your dress.
Wear your ironed dress and promise your boss you won't get pregnant (which in your case is predictable) and you like to type, and be sincere and wear your smile.
Find a job or get on welfare.
Borrow a child and get on welfare.
Borrow a child and stay in the house all day with the child, or go to the public park with the child and take the child to the welfare office and cry and say your man left you and be humble and wear your dress and your smile, and don't talk back, keep your dress on, cook more nice dinners, stay away from Telegraph Avenue, and still, you won't know the half of it, not in a million years.

How else? By making it known that it is possible to counteract fear and prejudice – I arranged for the theatre troupe Gay Sweatshop to take their play *Poppies* by Noel Greig to my old school. The school agreed, provided I talked beforehand to the sixth form about being gay and sexual politics – I did it (how could I not, I was frightened but I had to do it). The school survived and maybe it made a difference to some of those young people. You can send letters to people, like this letter a friend of mine sent.

Mr Richard Ebersol

Producer, *Saturday Night Live*

Dear Mr Ebersol,

On a recent *Saturday Night Live* broadcast, you presented a parody of Tennessee Williams' *Cat on a Hot Tin Roof* that stereo-typed, insulted and defamed gay people.

The gay man in this segment was depicted as stupid, weak, and pathetic. To protest sexual assault by a woman ('Maggie'), he was given lines like, 'I'm from San Francisco', 'I like to cook and dress up every Halloween as Marilyn Monroe', 'I have an alternative lifestyle', and finally 'I'm gay! I'm homosexual! I'm queer! I sleep with men! I'm a fag!' It is hard to believe you would broadcast a segment in which a Jew was being forced to celebrate Christmas and given lines like: 'I'm from Tel Aviv. I like shekels and yarmulkes! I'm a yid! A Kike!' Or one in which a black person was obliged to say: 'I'm from Harlem. I like grits and tap dancing. I'm a spade! A shine! A Coon!' Nor do I expect soon to see a skit in which the producing staff of *Saturday Night Live* is portrayed, and given lines like: 'I'm from Wall Street. I like power and poontang and dressing up as the Exterminator. I'm a fag-baiting, woman-hating, racist breeder slime!'

Yours,

A Concerned Viewer.[14]

You can try to effect change where you work, in your union give support to lesbian and gay initiatives or even suggest them your-self. Talk to friends. As Neil Bartlett beautifully said on TV last year, we all need friends, especially in times of crisis, and lesbians and gay men have always lived in times of crisis. We need friends who won't always collude with us, won't allow us to give in, who will be there to help us break the silence.

But the first place to start is with oneself. Ask the questions, break the silences within, express doubts and fears, learn to love all of yourself, including what is gay, and share it.

All of these things are hard, complex and challenging. It is not possible to do them all the time, but it is possible to attempt to integrate them into your life so that you can react on the spot when confronted. We are living in grim times and it is only by doing what we can, where we can, that we will survive. Survive to ensure that your gay children will be able to grow up true to themselves with a secure sense of their history and culture, without having, as I and all my gay brothers did, to rediscover it for themselves.

NOTES

This essay is a revised version of a talk given to the Men and Feminism Colloquium at St John's College, Cambridge, 15 May 1990.

1 This phrase is borrowed from Gregory Wood (Review of ed. G. Hanscombe: *Homosexuality*) in *New Statesman*, 30 October 1987.

2 'So' is gay slang for a lesbian or gay man, commonly used in the 1920s and 1930s.

3 This poem appears in the collection of poetry by Steve Cranfield and Martin Humphries, *Salt in Honey* (London: GMP, 1989).

4 Provisional statistics up to June 1991. Source: PHLS AIDS Centre, Communicable Disease Surveillance Centre, and Communicable Diseases (Scotland) Unit unpublished quarterly surveillance statistics, September 1991. When reading poem aloud please replace with the latest available data.

5 Louie Welch was the Republican candidate for Mayor of Houston, Texas September/October 1985. He didn't get elected.

6 Keith Hays is the leader of a campaign to prevent gay rights legislation from being passed by the New Zealand Parliament.

7 This is a reference to John Richards of Flint, Michigan, USA who spat in the face of two police officers and was charged with 'assault with attempt to murder.' (Observer 8.12.1985)

8 Quotation from *The Normal Heart*, a play by Larry Kramer (London: Methuen, 1986), 77.

9 Quotation from an early draft of the essay 'AIDS and the body of knowledge' by Pete Freer in *Heterosexuality* (London: GMP, 1987). The published version on page 66 reads: 'The body provides a multiplicity of sites on which desires can be played out.'

10 This poem appears in full in Carl Morse and Joan Larkin, eds, *Gay and Lesbian Poetry in Our Time* (New York: St Martin's Press, 1988).

11 See Carl Morse's introduction to Carl Morse and Joan Larkin, eds, *Gay and Lesbian Poetry in Our Time* (New York: St Martin's Press, 1988), xxiii–xxiv. For a more detailed examination of the issue of gay world views, see also, for example, Gloria Anzaldua, *Borderlands/La Frontera: The New Mestiza* (San Francisco: Spinsters/Aunt Lute Book Company, 1987); Judy Grahn, *Another Mother Tongue: Gay Words, Gay Worlds* (Boston: Beacon, 1984); and Harry Hay, 'Towards the New Frontiers of Fairy Vision . . . subject-SUBJECT Consciousness' in *RFD: A Country Journal for Gay Men Everywhere*, 24, 1980.

12 Jon Ward, 'The Nature of Heterosexuality' in Gillian E. Hanscombe and Martin Humphries, eds, *Heterosexuality* (London: GMP, 1987), 166.
13 This poem also appears in Morse and Larkin, eds, *Gay and Lesbian Poetry of Our Time*.
14 This letter is from *Impolite To My Butchers*, an unpublished play by Carl Morse, performed at Oval House, London and La Mama, La Galleria, New York.

Chapter 9

The personal, the political, the theoretical

The case of men's sexualities and sexual violences

Jeff Hearn

The relationship of men to feminism(s) is a difficult one: it is fundamentally about power, and is fundamentally problematic. The relationship exists within a social and societal context of men's domination in interpersonal relations and state, economic, cultural, educational, and other institutions, and yet it is not immediately obvious what the relationship might mean or include. It would seem to encompass material social relations between feminists and men, as well as feminist critiques of and challenges to men,[1] and men's responses, particularly conscious responses, to feminism.

There is also the question of diversity. None of the elements just mentioned is itself unified. For example, the 'feminist critiques' of men are wide-ranging.[2] In their 1969 manifesto, the New York-based Redstockings wrote:

> In reality, every such relationship [between a woman and a man] is a *class* relationship, and the conflicts between individual men and women are political conflicts that can only be solved collectively . . . .
>
> We regard our personal experience, and our feelings about that experience, as the basis for an analysis of our common situation. We cannot rely on existing ideologies as they are all products of a male supremacist culture. We question every generalization and accept none that is not confirmed by our experience . . . .
>
> We identify with all women. We define our best interests as that of the poorest, most brutally exploited woman . . . .
>
> In fighting for our liberation we will always take the side of

women against their oppressors. We will not ask what is 'revolutionary' or 'reformist', only what is good for women.

(598–601; emphasis in original)

In contrast, Annie Leclerc advises women:

One must not wage war on men. That is his way of attaining value. Deny in order to affirm. Kill to love. One must simply deflate his values with the needle of ridicule.

(79)

A third problematic issue for the relationship of men to feminism is the definitional one – for if feminism is theory and practice by women for women, then men cannot be feminists, even though men can learn from, agree with, respond to, be changed by feminism. So in talking of men and feminism I am referring to a relationship of *difference*, and a difference of a different type and order to, say, economic class relations or age relations or international relations.

A fourth reason for the problematic nature of the relationship of men and feminism is that while feminism sets out challenges and questions for men, those challenges and questions *cannot simply be answered in some complete or definitive way*. Whatever is done or said by men in response to feminism, further questions and challenges, perhaps different ones, remain. The whole notion of how we (men) reply and respond to feminism is itself problematic: there would seem to be an epistemological break between the questions and the answers, as if the latter are always answering slightly (or not so slightly) different questions or answering them in slightly (or not so slightly) irrelevant ways. In light of this, forms of silence may at times be the most appropriate or most informative response.[3]

A rather different way of expressing some of these difficulties is in terms of the feminist principle, 'the personal is political.' The phrase has been an important and enduring one in the Women's Liberation Movement, and although it is open to a variety of interpretations,[4] it refers partly to the connectedness of experience: subjective/objective; private/public; practice/theory; personal/political. Men's responses to feminism are also personal and political. When we attempt to respond to feminism personally or politically, we are also responding politically or personally (respectively), whatever we might suppose. We cannot just answer in some disinterested "neutral" mode – we are always implicated and located; we are always part of the answering. Or to put it another way, (our) discourse is always embodied.

By extension, the personal is not only political but also theoretical – the personal is political is theoretical.[5] Our (men's) responses to feminism need to be, indeed are, personal, political, theoretical, even if we don't realize that in any conscious way.

Since the late sixties and early seventies, there has been a whole range of broadly positive responses by men to feminism. Personal responses have included changes in personal relationships; talking more directly, honestly, emotionally and in other ways to women and men; changing practices in child-care and in housework; meeting with other men on a more intimate basis; the formation of men's groups. In one sense these are all political responses too, but there have also been more deliberate public political responses such as the formation of men's anti-sexist organizations like the National Organization for Changing Men (NOCM) and the National Organization of Men Against Sexism (NOMAS) in the United States, Men Against Sexism networks in the UK and a variety of publicly visible men's groups and organizations engaged in political campaigning, writing, film-making, performance and so on. As before, such public political initiatives are, of course, also personal matters. Both personal and political responses are themselves theoretical, in the sense that they represent the application, whether explicit or implicit, of practical and political theorizing. More explicitly theoretical responses include academic and political study, research and writing of a more extended and generalized nature. An early British example of this was Andrew Tolson's *The Limits of Masculinity*. Such theoretical initiatives are also political and personal, and have indeed been developed by those involved in men's groups and the other anti-sexist activities.

There are clearly many connections between the personal, the political and the theoretical; in order to narrow the field a little, I will focus here on men's positive, that is, anti-sexist and pro-feminist, responses to feminism in one particular personal, political, and theoretical area, that of men's sexualities and sexual violences.

THE PERSONAL

Men's personal responses to feminism are immensely various – they are often hostile, occasionally positive, frequently ambivalent. They are rarely, however, discussed in terms of sexuality and sexual violence. One of the insistent difficulties here is, of course, the dominant definition of sexuality as a private matter. For men who have made or have attempted to make positive responses to feminism in this area, the explicit focus has usually been on reworking men's power relations, first with women, and second with other men. This may take the form of trying to break established sexual patterns of objectification, fixation, and conquest, particularly with women;[6] it may also take the form of trying to develop different ways of relating sexually to each other as men. This might involve showing more physical and emotional affection to men, and it might involve forming sexual relations with men that are less based on domination and oppression.[7] For some men, and this appeared to be particularly the case in the early years of Men Against Sexism activities in the seventies, responding positively to feminism meant taking up sexual relations with men as a political act, even if they did not necessarily or initially feel erotically attracted to men. For some men, responding positively to feminism has meant acknowledging bisexuality, or developing self-defined autonomous sexuality, or assuming celibacy, or even celebrating heterosexuality as positive.

In light of this variety, attempts at generalization are difficult, even if sexuality is acknowledged as a site of power. There are, however, a number of further complications. From my experience of being in men's groups, one of the issues that often prompts men's initial involvement in such groups is a disjunction between a political/public/intellectual support for feminism and the immediate difficulties of their lives through sexual conflicts, separation, divorce, infidelity and so on. A second problem is that the privateness of certain kinds of sexual activity means that the relationship between what men say (in men's groups, for example), feel and do about sexuality is not clear. Thirdly, and most worryingly, it is certainly possible for men to be involved in men's groups and continue to be sexually violent. When some years ago it was discovered that one of the men in the men's group I was in was hitting the woman he lived with, the other members of the group were in complete disagreement about whether to exclude him or whether to work with him on stopping the violence – a dilemma that I think illustrates the problem of the relationship of men in men's groups to other men in the community.[8]

In view of these difficulties and appropriately as a mode of looking at the personal, I'll talk briefly on my own personal experience. If I look at my own *personal* responses to feminism, one of the interesting things to me is that I haven't in the past thought about them *initially* in terms of sexuality and sexual violence (even though these issues have been central in my more theoretical analysis). For example, if asked to describe my own motivation for becoming involved in men's groups, child-care campaigning, and other anti-sexist activities from 1978 onwards, I have usually spoken of my principled support for feminism and opposition to men's oppression of women, intense concern – and exhaustion – with child-care through my experience of living with young children, and feelings of unease about being a man. Looking back now fourteen years on I can fairly easily reformulate my involvement in these activities in terms of sexual issues that were important to me then – what I felt sexually; what I did sexually or would like to have done; who or what I desired; the relationship of pleasure, pain and sexuality.

The first of these sexual issues was a movement from a taken-for-granted heterosexuality towards a critical stance on it. This was partly a matter of my changing attitude towards heterosexuality from the seventies into the eighties – both in the sense of realizing that heterosexuality isn't just normal or natural but that it is socially constructed, and that this doesn't just apply in some general societal way but also applies to me. So I began thinking about heterosexuality and my own sexuality in quite different ways, in which what I did seemed more changeable, in some ways, more superficial. Writing in 1981, I concluded that 'control of reproduction (by men) . . . necessitates a heterosexual and heterosexist ideology [in order to] maintain that control and to display it' (*Birth and Afterbirth* 50). It was also a matter of my changing practice, including a reduction in the importance of 'sex' and a movement away from intercourse, as well as real uncertainties and confusions about what to do sexually.

This linked with more general uncertainties about how to develop a long-term relationship with a woman in the context of feminism.[9] Very simply, there were no longer any pre-given answers on how that might be done or attempted. In some ways, all the available models seem flawed. It would be wrong to see such uncertainty as an intellectual or even an attitudinal issue. Reworking sexuality was very much a practical matter: there were clear lived connections, for example, between the decline of 'sex' and the sheer exhaustion of child-care. As I wrote in 1979, '"Too tired for sex" is a cliché usually applied to wives inventing excuses for overly insistent husbands; in my experience the toll of three children can mean that the cliché can certainly apply to men' (*Birth* 25).

There were also more subtle connections between my everyday life and sexual life. One that I still don't feel completely clear on is how child-care brought from me not just a practical but also a very emotional response. It was as if living with young children gave me a justification for being much more emotional, particularly in terms of crying more. This kind of emotionality was, however, intermingled with the greater range of emotional expression that I also found in men's groups, and in turn both of these emotional (or emotionalized) experiences were (and probably are still) mixed up with my becoming much more emotional about sexual desires. What I mean by this last point is that I didn't necessarily experience greater sexual desire (in fact, it was often less), but that my emotional feelings around sexuality were more intense.

It is important to add that my experience of these and other sexual issues, and their interrelationships, was at that time often complicated and ambivalent. It involved tensions, internal and interpersonal conflicts, issues of my/men's power, as well as mutual pleasures. It raised many questions and frequently a simple lack of answers.

Since then my relationship to feminism has changed. I have continued to be involved in men's groups, and anti-sexist activities and campaigns. Having been for many years 'anti-therapy,' I decided in 1984 to try psychoanalysis, partly to work on sexual issues. These and other experiences have made me aware of the importance of the range of sexualities and the importance of opposing sexual violences in all their forms. I have become increasingly aware how much of my own social life can be understood in terms of underlying sexual themes, and yet how such themes are themselves rarely coherent, solid phenomena, but rather are more usually fleeting and contradictory. Current issues include the continuation of a long-term heterosexual relationship, the virtual rejection of heterosexual intercourse, and the acknowledgement of the importance for me of celibacy, narcissism, masturbation, gayness and my positive relationship with gay men. Sexuality can just as much involve celibacy or narcissism as heterosexuality or gayness, yet for some reason this is rarely talked about. Then there's the question that I/we feel differently at different times; additionally, such 'types' of sexuality often exist by including elements of other 'types' within them. As Irigaray makes clear, the very idea of heterosexuality relies on homosexual/homosocial relations and exchange between men.[10] My (and other men's) relationship to men and men's groups can partly be understood as an activity on a 'gay continuum.'[11] I remain in a heterosexual relationship and yet experience daily the oppression of heterosexual expectations, partly because the dominant models of heterosexuality are so oppressive, and partly because heterosexuality is only one aspect, albeit an important aspect, of me.

With all this has come the rejection of the idea of sexual *orientation* or of *possessing* a specific sexuality. I also have real doubts about the meaningfulness of the three main categories of orientation – 'heterosexual/straight,' 'gay,' 'bisexual' – as descriptions of 'orientation.' I now recognize a more fragmented, yet more definite, sexual 'identity' that includes elements that are mainly heterosexual, but also gay, celibate and narcissistic – a kind of clear fuzziness – that acknowledges the importance of overlapping, rather than unproblematic identifications.[12] I am now inclined to think that most, or perhaps even all, men carry around such diverse sexual elements; indeed my daily experience confirms this.

THE POLITICAL

What do men's political responses to feminism in terms of sexuality and sexual violence look like? As already noted, personal responses are also political – they involve power. If, however, we turn to public political responses, the picture is somewhat different – for overall there has been relatively little overt political action by men around sexuality and sexual violence, *as a positive response to feminism*. Instead there has been much confusion.

Positive political responses have generally been developed either proactively (that is, through our own initiative and self-direction) or reactively (in reaction to specific demands or issues raised by others) towards women's and (particular forms of) men's sexualities. Men's proactive responses have included a general principled support for Women's Liberation and feminism,[13] including by implication the demands of the Women's Liberation Movement, such as demands for woman-defined autonomous sexuality for women, the rights of lesbians, women's reproductive rights, freedom from sexual violence, and legal reforms. While this can be seen as a positive relationship to feminism in terms of women's sexuality, there has been little detailed political response beyond that.

Paralleling some men's positive relation to the Women's Movement in the form of anti-sexist groups, networks, and campaigns has been some men's proactive relation to men and men's sexuality. This appears most obviously in the Gay Liberation Movement and gay-affirmative support from anti-sexist men, heterosexual or otherwise. In saying this, it is important to acknowledge that gay (men's) liberation has not necessarily been pro-feminist; this has been discussed by feminists in relation to the political, organizing and academic analysis of some gay men.[14] Indeed, divisions between gay men and lesbians on issues of gay male sexism, among others, was one of the reasons for the break-up of the Gay Liberation Front in the early seventies.

I see support by heterosexual-identified men for gay men as particularly important for a number of reasons. There are liberal reasons, such as the promotion of principles of equality and justice; radical reasons around the gendered transformations and liberation of society; and selfish reasons which relate to the acknowledgement of both the gay part of men and the possibility of changing sexuality in the future. However, as with principled support for Women's Liberation, principled political support for Gay Liberation and for bisexuality has usually been couched in fairly general statements without much attention to specific political activities. Whatever the nature of pro-feminist men's principled support for gay liberation, divisions between gay men and heterosexual men have been a significant theme over the last twenty years. In 1973 an article in *Brothers Against Sexism* argued that 'Coming out is the only way forward,' as 'straight men derive privileges from being straight as such' (17). This demand from some gay men was a key issue at a men's conference held in London in November 1974. This culminated in several gay men walking out after accusing the 'straights' of homophobia. The plenary session was dominated by some gay men angrily telling the 'straights' to come out or shut up.[15]

While such splits have rarely occurred so dramatically since, the existence of different interests and tensions around men's sexuality has certainly remained within and around men's anti-sexist activity. While some gay men have kept away from such 'anti-sexist organizing,' others have been a clear presence. Relations between gay men and 'non-gay men' have been an important issue within men's anti-sexist organizing, even though gay organizing and anti-sexist organizing have involved, in the main, different groups of men at any particular time.[16]

On the other hand, some men have argued for the celebration of men as men regardless of their sexuality, a pro-male rather than pro-feminist stance. But a professed commitment to 'men's (or male) liberation' can easily blur into the pursuit of 'men's rights' at the expense of women, as in the case of the Coalition of Free Men in the United States, a pro-male and frequently anti-feminist organization.[17] It seems that some men become interested and involved in sexual politics or even anti-sexism, and then at some point in their journey get hooked into an individual or collective narcissism. It is as if they get stuck in an emotional swamp along the side of the road. Some men even balance such a celebration of 'maleness' that is clearly homoerotic with a masterful heterosexual identification, thereby constituting one particular manifestation of the 'new man.' In any case, the 'pro-male' attitude clearly serves as an excuse for many to reproduce or develop their misogyny.

Another rather different and relatively recent strand among some 'anti-sexist' men has been the development of a more spiritual 'male-centered' approach to masculinity and sexuality. This has sometimes focused on the exploration of positive archetypes, such as the 'wild man' and the 'horned god.'[18] Recent weekends and workshops have included such titles as 'Everyman,' 'Fatherspace,' 'Rites of passage for men,' 'Becoming men,' 'Men moving together,' 'The inner and outer world of maleness,' and 'Man to man'.[19] In a different way to the previous, this approach celebrates men, drawing on traditions from religion, paganism, mythology, initiation rituals, pre-industrial society,

'Nature,' 'earth,' transpersonal psychology and (post)Reichian bodywork (that is, therapeutic work on the body). Exploring masculinity and sexuality in such 'depth' raises a number of contradictory issues – is it re-asserting a biological or spiritual essentialism? is it deconstructing masculinity? is it about regaining or losing power? is it about sexuality between men? My guess is that probably all these elements may be present in this kind of organizing. While men may come together as friends or in men's groups, or in some other way, public men-only organizing that excludes women always has to be viewed with some doubts and ambivalence, for it may bring together and be based on both radical pro-feminist and anti-feminist sentiments.

The truth is that while sexuality is certainly an important *implicit* issue in men's political relation to feminism, it has rarely been an *explicit* central organizing political principle in that relation. Apart from pro-feminist gay organizing, a possible exception to this is the tendency in the UK that has clustered around Achilles Heel, the men's anti-sexist publishing collective that has produced the magazine of the same name since 1978.[20] This is most clearly seen in the special double issue of the magazine numbers 6 and 7 published in 1982–83, and in Metcalf and Humphries's edited collection, *The Sexuality of Men*, which includes several contributions from members or friends of the collective.

An emphasis on sexuality has also been important more recently in the statements of the Men, Masculinities and Socialism Group, to which I have belonged since 1989.[21] This group has attempted to build an analysis that recognizes the centrality of sexuality but not as something strictly separate from other oppressions. Thus a typical statement reads: 'We want to emphasise ... the sheer variety of masculine forms. These complex and often contradictory forms and relations are there in the specific histories of black, gay, bisexual, class-related, disabled, able-bodied, young, old, regional [and other] masculinities' (18). These political complexities have their equivalents in theoretical analysis of the deconstruction of the 'monolithic' category of men.[22]

What has been much more typical than a proactive approach to sexualities has been a reactive stance against particular forms of sexual oppression, as with that against masculinist sexuality taken by the Achilles Heel collective or in Dansky *et al.*'s

'Effeminist Manifesto.' The reactive position is clearest with respect to men's sexual violence. This includes numerous campaigns and projects against pornography, rape, and sexual harassment, as well as anti-violence counselling projects, focusing largely on men's violence towards women.[23]

Then there are those politics that have grown reactively to anti-homosexual politics, particularly in response to the impact of HIV/AIDS in some gay male communities. The most obvious recent example in the UK is the range of campaigning against Clause 28 of the Local Government Bill, including both local organizing and mass rallies in Manchester, London and elsewhere. This 1988 legislation is a clear governmental response to the constructed association of HIV/AIDS and gay men; as such, it represents the most pernicious legislative attack on lesbian and gay rights since the nineteenth century. Specifically, Clause 28 prohibits local authorities from 'promoting homosexuality,' publishing any material that might have this effect, or promoting the teaching, in any maintained school, of the acceptability of 'homosexuality' as a 'pretended family relationship.' A subclause stipulates that these conditions should not 'prohibit the doing of anything for the purpose of treating or preventing the spread of disease' – a clear implicit reference to HIV/AIDS. Since the passage of the Clause, opposition has continued through Stonewall and other organizations, and the law itself has been shown to be logically confused and not as effective in its original aims as its drafters intended. Indeed, there is also an argument that 'Clause 28' paradoxically has brought homosexuality more fully into public debate, and even that it has in some cases indirectly assisted in publicizing the civil rights of lesbians and gay men to local authority services.[24] Furthermore, recent evidence suggests that in the UK many gay men have responded to HIV/AIDS with 'safer sex' practices. Heterosexuals, in contrast, have done far less to protect themselves, and it is therefore among this 'community' that sero-positive conversion rates are increasing relatively rapidly.

In summary, men's political responses to feminism – outside of gay liberationism and gay organizing – have generally been limited by abstraction and over-generality, reactivity rather than proactivity, and doubts about the possibility of change. There have also been specific aspects of sexuality and sexual violence that have been neglected in men's political responses to feminism

– perhaps most notably, the abuse and molestation of children, men's sexuality in organizations, and the relationship of sexuality and other oppressions.[25]

THE THEORETICAL

What about men's positive theoretical responses to sexuality and sexual violence? (Before going into these, I should perhaps make it clear that attention to 'the theoretical' is not some impersonal, remote activity; it is a very personal and engaged matter. This applies both in the sense that personal and political aspects are important in the construction of (good) theory in this area, and in my own personal involvement in constructing theory, on my own and collectively.) Sexuality has been widely invoked in theoretical debates both as *a topic and category for analysis* and as *a fundamental basis of discourse*. On the first count, 'sexuality' refers to men's (or 'male') sexuality, sexual relations, and the particular types of sexuality of particular men. In the seventies, the most influential work in these areas was script theory, showing the learned social construction of sexuality; and gay theory, establishing the significance of different forms of men's sexuality. The first of these two has, along with 'sex role' theory more generally, been important in the development of what has come to be called 'Men's Studies' within the academy.[26]

More recent years have seen a definite development of more critical work by men on sexuality. In one important article, Carrigan, Connell and Lee made a number of conceptual advances on previous thinking: the recognition of the *general* relevance of gay theory for an understanding of men's sexuality and not just those men identified as gay; the contribution of psychoanalysis, particularly towards an understanding of contradictions in masculinity; and the conceptualization of hegemonic masculinity, that is, of the dominant and dominating forms of masculinities that to some extent set the normative agenda for the evaluation of other masculinities (551–604). I see all these insights as important, and indeed it is gradually becoming more accepted that gay, psychoanalytic, and anti-hegemonic theorizing has to be attended to in analyzing men's sexuality, even if these contributions are themselves subject to critique. It is partly through these influences that writers have recognized the need to develop explicitly critical studies on men and masculinities, rather than just the expansion of 'Men's Studies.'[27]

A major focus of recent critical theorizing has been on men's heterosexuality and heterosexual men. This has been primarily in terms of issues of power and domination as, for example, in Blye Frank's work on the historical and social construction of 'hegemonic heterosexual masculinity,' in which he addresses the way 'hegemonic masculinity' is characteristically 'heterosexual' at the level of social structure as well as interpersonal relations. This approach has some parallels with the concept of 'hierarchic heterosexuality' that I develop in *The Gender of Oppression*. Dominant forms of heterosexuality, I argue here, are premised upon social inequalities of power between women and men; as such, hierarchic heterosexuality is one of the basic institutions of patriarchy, not just at the level of social structure, but also in the material relations of bodies and personal sexual practices. Other analyses have linked an understanding of heterosexual men in terms of their own homosociability (or even homosexuality), thus offering the possibility of relating power dynamics between women and men with those *between men*.[28] Paradoxically, another, and probably equally significant, facet of this kind of theorizing focuses on the interrelationship between heterosexual masculinity and homophobia.[29] All of these theoretical approaches seem to me important in understanding men's sexualities and sexual violences, and all in different ways speak to my own experience.

The themes of power and domination have also been explored at the more micro level in Jack Litewka's classic statement of the 'socialized penis' and the dominant script of objectification/fixation/conquest in men's sexual activity (16–35). A crucial issue here is the paradox of the social construction of the supposed 'uncontrollability' of men's sexualities, a framework introduced by Coveney *et al.* and further developed by Howard Buchbinder, who details the difficulties for men of breaking the connection between 'power' and 'pleasure,' while also noting the extreme variability of men's experiences.

Another major focus in critical work has been on sexual violence, and perhaps most notably on pornography. Recent theoretical work on pornography takes on the alienation of 'male sexuality' in pornographic consumption, oppositions between activity and passivity and between objectification and subjectification, and the relationship of pornography, homophobia and gay sexuality.[30] Both Andy Moye and Tim Beneke note some of the ways in which pornography may operate for men by breaking certain stereotypical rules; for example, by appealing to the man as a passive consumer, or by giving some women actors in pornography a degree of subjectivity in contrast to their dominant objectification. Much of this work links directly with more general theoretical work in which sexuality isn't just a topic but is (a basis of) discourse itself. A similar connection can be observed in much recent work on men's bodies and the embodiment of masculinity.[31]

This leads into a second aspect of men's theoretical responses to feminism in which sexuality isn't just a topic but is rather a fundamental basis of discourse. This approach draws on a variety of forms of feminist theorizing, including those which argue for sexuality as the basis of gender, heterosexuality as the basis of hierarchy, and the sexually encoded nature of discourse.[32] This last theme has been taken up by Victor Seidler, who has written on the falsity of Enlightenment divisions between reason and desire, and on the relation of that division to masculinity and power. Tim Edwards has raised questions on the relation of homosexuality and social theory more generally, and articulated some of the possible tensions between feminism and gay sexuality.

Others have focused on more specific discourses – on 'male sexual narrative' in the media, the 'homosexual subtext in film,' 'organization sexuality,' 'the sexuality of organization,' and 'the need to eroticize academic labour.'[33] Much work remains to be done applying this kind of approach to other areas and 'disciplines,' such as history and economics.

In all this theoretical work, sexuality is recognized as one of the main bases of men's domination of what is sometimes called 'patriarchy.' As such, men's theoretical responses to feminism on sexuality and sexual violence recognize sexuality as a fundamental oppression of women by men, as well as a major source of difference between men.

CONCLUSION

In many ways all three of these perspectives – the personal, the political, and the theoretical – are about the same issues. They all involve practice; all refer to power and the oppression of women; all suggest the importance of changing men's relations, including relations of sexuality, with both women and other men; and they all relate to each other.

On the other hand, these perspectives also show the importance of complexities, contradictions, ambiguities, and inconsistencies. And there are definite differences, too, arising from the unique experiences of individual men, men's apparent difficulty in organizing concrete and proactive political initiatives around sexuality, and real uncertainties concerning the interrelationship of sexuality, social theory, and theorizing.

After all, the very separation of the personal, the political, and the theoretical in malestream discourse is questionable; it may itself be a feature of dominant forms of men's sexuality that needs to be challenged and undermined. The separation of perspectives that I've used here, then, even in its modified form, without question raises definite difficulties. Perhaps if I were to start writing this essay again I would take a selection of issues around sexuality and sexual violence, and attempt to explore the personal, political and theoretical all at the same time. This could be done for such issues as the relationship of heterosexuality and homosexuality, the deconstruction of the notion of 'sexual orientation,' the discursive analysis of the idea of 'sexuality' itself, the significance of the visual in sexual experience, the embodiment of sexuality, the relationship of sexuality and sexual violence. To put this another way, the personal is political is theoretical.

Having said that, more fundamental problems remain around the different kinds of attempts to articulate written discourses on men and sexuality. For example, if discourse, including personal, political, theoretical (and other) discourses, is sexually encoded, then talking about sexuality will involve *both* saying and showing sexuality. There are also clear difficulties in the extent to which we, men, can speak of our own sexualities and sexual violences, if one of the ways they exist, persist, and are known is through the experience, the subjective experience, of those who are affected by them – women, children, young people, and indeed other men. In this last respect, men's sexual subjectivities of each other, gay or otherwise, are particularly important in the development of sexual theory. Another sort of problem is the extent to which men's sexualities and sexual violences can be separated off from other aspects of life and experience. Thus future work by men, whether personal, political, or theoretical, needs to 'talk the body' in order to overcome the separations of body/mind, sexuality/rationality and subjectivity/objectivity that are reproduced in dominant forms of masculinities. Finally, future work must also attend to the interrelations of men's sexualities and sexual violences to other social divisions and oppressions – age, class, (dis)ability, ethnicity/'race' – through which men are defined, constructed and categorized. Perhaps it will be precisely the diversity of voices that can be brought to bear on the issues at hand that will prove most effective in transforming the legacy of sexual power.

NOTES

I am grateful to participants at the colloquium, and in particular Harry Ferguson and David Morgan, for their comments on this presentation, and to Sue Moody for typing the script.

 1 See, for example, Friedman and Sarah, 1982.
 2 For further discussion of the diversity of feminist critiques of men, see Hearn, *The Gender of Oppression*, pp. 21–25.
 3 Examples of such possible epistemological breaks can be found throughout Jardine and Smith's *Men in Feminism*.
 4 See, for example, Elshtain, 1981; Stanley and Wise, 1983.
 5 See Hearn, 1987, ch. 1. A fuller version would be 'The personal is material is political is theoretical.'
 6 See Betzold, 1977; Buchbinder, 1987.
 7 While the association of heterosexuality and domination is well documented (Buchbinder *et al.*, 1987), the association of gay (men's) sexuality and domination is a much more complicated and controversial question. Relevant issues include the importation of 'heterosexual' patterns in gay relations and gay culture, as in the phenomenon of 'gay macho' (Kinsman, 1987), and the overarching similarities of gay men and heterosexual men, for example, in the separation of sex and loving emotion (Coveney *et al.*, 1984).
 8 See Hearn, 1987, p. 13.
 9 For a discussion of this issue see Metcalf and Morrison, 1983.
10 Irigaray 1985, chapter 9.
11 See Rich, 1980.
12 The term 'fuzzy' is used by the Movement for a New Society, 1977, p. 110, to refer to some of these overlapping identifications, in particular the experience of the oppression of heterosexual expectations.
13 Two different kinds of principled statements of support are those on the 'commitments' (Commitments Collective, 1980) and a minimum self-definition of the anti-sexist men's movement (Morrison, 1980). Commentaries on these are given by Rowan, 1987; Hearn, 1987; Cooper, 1990.

14 See Stanley, 1984.

15 Conference Report, 1975, cited in Cooper, 1990.

16 See Humphries, 1987.

17 A useful summary of some of the problems of this approach is provided by Baker, 1991.

18 See, respectively, Bly, 1988 and Rowan, 1987.

19 These titles of workshops are taken from announcements in the Leamington-based magazine, *Men for Change* (1990) Nos. 14 and 15.

20 Achilles Heel was a London-based men's anti-sexist and socialist publishing collective that produced the magazine of the same name from 1978 to 1983, and again in 1987, as well as three pamphlets. The magazine was relaunched in 1990 by a collective based in Sheffield and London.

21 The Men, Masculinities and Socialism Group is an autonomous policy group of the Socialist Movement. The group included members in Leamington, Liverpool, London, Nottingham, Sheffield and elsewhere and organized the 'Changing Men, Changing Politics' Event in Sheffield, October 1990. Following on this event, a day meeting was held in Nottingham in April 1992 under the title 'Gay, Bisexual and Heterosexual Men Combine for Action.' The meeting included workshops on 'Bisexuality', 'Homophobia', 'The personal and political in defining our own sexuality', 'Stonewall postal action network (and other anti-Section 28 action)', 'Gay legal aid', 'Men's health', 'Men overcoming violence (Nottingham)' and 'Images of men in the media'.

22 See Hearn and Collinson, 1990.

23 Specific projects include Men Against Pornography in Leeds and New York, Men Against Rape, and men's support for the Campaign Against Pornography and Censorship. Gondolf documents a number of anti-violence counselling projects (e.g. EMERGE and RAVEN) in the United States; *Der Spiegel*, 1986 reports on Männer Gegen Männer-Gewalt (Men Against Male Violence) activities in Germany; works by Mason and by Waring and Wilson discuss the activities of Men Overcoming Violence (MOVE) in the UK.

24 A very useful survey of the interpretations and impact of the 'Clause' is given in Evans, 1989/90.

25 On child abuse see Hearn, 1990a; on men's sexuality at work see Hearn, 1985. Mercer and Julien, 1988 discuss the relationship of sexuality and racism from the perspective of black gay men.

26 The emerging field of 'Men's Studies', though nominally parallel with Women's Studies, includes writings by and about men that vary widely in their attitude towards feminism and their commitment to a critical perspective, and that are generally set within traditional social science frameworks.

27 See Hearn, 1989a, 1989b; and several chapters in Hearn and Morgan, 1990.

28 See Seidenberg, 1970; Irigaray, 1985; Hearn, 1992.

29 See Herek, 1986.

30 See, respectively, Brod, 1984 and 1990; Moye, 1985; Beneke, 1990; and Stoltenberg, 1990a and 1990b.

31 See Connell, 1983 and 1987; Brittan, 1989; Jackson, 1990; Hearn, 1990b.
32 See, respectively, MacKinnon, 1982; Zita, 1982; and Grosz, 1987.
33 See, respectively, Dyer, 1985; Wood, 1987; Hearn and Parkin, 1987, and Hearn, 1992; Burrell and Hearn, 1989; and Burrell, 1984.

REFERENCES

Achilles Heel (1982–83), Special Issue on Sexuality, 6 and 7.

Anon (1986) 'Sheffield Men Against Sexual Harassment,' *Men's Antisexist Newsletter*, 23.

Baker, Peter (1991) 'Are men right about men's rights?' *Cosmopolitan*, July, 10–14.

Beneke, Timothy (1990) 'Intrusive images and subjectified bodies: notes on visual heterosexual porn,' in Michael Kimmel, ed. *Men Confront Pornography*, Crown, New York, 168–87.

Betzold, Michael (1977) 'How pornography shackles men and oppresses women' in Jon Snodgrass, ed. *A Book of Readings for Men Against Sexism*, Times Change, Albion, Ca.

Bly, Robert (1988) 'The mystery of the wild man,' *Resurgence* 128, May–June 8–10.

Braidotti, Rosa (1987) 'Envy: or with my brains and your looks' in Alice Jardine and Paul Smith, eds, *Men in Feminism*, Methuen, New York, 233–41.

Brittan, Arthur (1989) *Masculinity and Power*, Blackwell, Oxford/New York.

Brod, Harry (1984) 'Eros Thanatised: pornography and male sexuality,' *Humanities in Society* 7, Winter–Spring.

—— (1990) 'Pornography and the alienation of male sexuality' in Jeff Hearn and David H.J. Morgan, eds, *Men, Masculinities and Social Theory*, Unwin Hyman, London, 124–39.

Buchbinder, Howard (1987) 'Male heterosexuality. The socialized penis revisited' in Howard Buchbinder *et al.*, eds, *Who's on Top? The Politics of Heterosexuality*, Garamond, Toronto, 63–82.

Buchbinder, Howard, Varda Burstyn, Dinah Forbes and Mercedes Steadman (1987) *Who's On Top? The Politics of Heterosexuality*, Garamond, Toronto.

Burrell, Gibson (1984) 'Sex and organizational analysis,' *Organization Studies*, 5.2, 97–118.

Burrell, Gibson and Jeff Hearn (1989) 'The sexuality of organization' in Hearn *et al.*, eds, *The Sexuality of Organization*, Sage, London, 1–28.

Carrigan, Tim, R.W. Connell and John Lee (1985) 'Toward a new sociology of masculinity,' *Theory and Society* 14.5, 551–604.

'Coming out is the only way forward,' *Brothers Against Sexism*, 3, 17.

Commitments Collective (1980) 'Anti-sexist commitments for men – draught (sic)3,' *Anti-Sexist Men's Newsletter* 9, 17–18.

Conference Report (1975) *Men Against Sexism or the Pigs' Last Grunt*, 4.

Connell, R.W. (1983) *Which Way Is Up?* Allen & Unwin, Sydney.

—— (1987) *Gender and Power*, Polity, Cambridge.

Cooper, Mick (1990) *A Critical History of the Men's Movement*, Achilles Heel, Sheffield.

Coveney, Lal, Margaret Jackson, Sheila Jeffreys, Leslie Kaye, Pat Mahoney (1984) *The Sexuality Papers: Male Sexuality and the Social Control of Women*, Hutchinson, London.

Dansky, Steve, John Knoebel, Kenneth Pitchford (1977) 'The Effeminist Manifesto' in Jon Snodgrass, ed., *A Book of Readings for Men Against Sexism*, Times Change, Albion, Ca. 116–20.

Dyer, Richard (1985) 'Male sexuality in the media' in Andy Metcalf and Martin Humphries, eds, *The Sexuality of Men*, Pluto, London, 28–43.

Edwards, Tim (1990) 'Beyond sex and gender: masculinity, homosexuality and social theory' in Jeff Hearn and David H.J. Morgan, eds, *Men, Masculinities and Social Theory*, Unwin Hyman, London, 110–23.

Elshtain, Jean Bethke (1981) *Public Man, Private Woman*, Martin Robertson, Oxford.

Evans, David T. (1989/90) 'Section 28: law, myth and paradox,' *Critical Social Policy*, No. 27, 19(3), 73–95.

Frank, Blye (1987) 'Hegemonic heterosexual masculinity,' *Studies in Political Economy*, 24, 159–70.

Friedman, Scarlet and Elizabeth Sarah, eds, (1982) *On the Problem of Men: Two Feminist Conferences*, Women's Press, London.

Gondolf, Edward W. (1985) *Men Who Batter: An Integrated Approach for Stopping Wife Abuse*, Learning Publications, Holmes Beach, Fl.

Grosz, Elizabeth (1987) 'Feminist theory and the challenges to knowledge,' *Women's Studies International Forum*, 10(5), 475–80.

Hanmer, Jalna (1990) 'Men, power and the exploitation of women' in Jeff Hearn and David H.J. Morgan, eds, *Men, Masculinities and Social Theory*, Unwin Hyman, London, 21–42.

Hearn, Jeff (1983) *Birth and Afterbirth: A Materialist Account*, Achilles Heel, London.

—— (1985) 'Men's sexuality at work' in Andy Metcalf and Martin Humphries, eds, *The Sexuality of Men*, Pluto, London, 110–28.

—— (1987) *The Gender of Oppression: Men, Masculinity and the Critique of Marxism*, Wheatsheaf, Brighton.

—— (1989a) *Some Sociological Issues in Researching Men and Masculinities*, Hallsworth Research Fellowship Working Paper No. 2, Department of Social Policy and Social Work, University of Manchester, Manchester.

—— (1989b) 'Reviewing men and masculinities – or mostly boys' own papers,' *Theory, Culture and Society*, 6(4), 665–89.

—— (1990a) '"Child abuse" and men's violence' in Violence Against Children Study Group, *Taking Child Abuse Seriously*, Unwin Hyman, London, 63–85.

—— (1990b) 'Recent developments in the critical studies of men and masculinities – or trying to talk our bodies.' Paper at Kropp og Kjonn (The Body and Gender) Seminar, Norwegian Network for Research on Men, Oslo. Mimeo. University of Bradford forthcoming in the Report of the Conference.

—— (1992), *Men in the Public Eye: The Construction and Deconstruction of Public Men and Public Masculinities*, Routledge, London.

Hearn, Jeff and David Collinson (1990) 'Unities and divisions between men and masculinities (l) The categories of men and the case of sociology,' British Sociological Association Annual Conference 'Social Divisions and Change,' University of Surrey, April. Mimeo. University of Bradford.

Hearn, Jeff and David H.J. Morgan, eds, (1990) *Men, Masculinities and Social Theory*, Unwin Hyman, London.

Hearn, Jeff and Wendy Parkin (1987) *'Sex' at 'Work': The Power and Paradox of Organization Sexuality*, Wheatsheaf, Brighton.

Herek, Gregory (1987) 'On heterosexual masculinity: some psychological consequences of the social construction of gender and sexuality,' *American Behavioral Scientist*, 29(5), 563–77.

Humphries, Martin (1987) 'Choosing with care: working with non-gay men' in Gillian E. Hanscombe and Martin Humphries, eds, *Heterosexuality*, GMP, London, 86–95.

Irigaray, Luce (1985) *This Sex Which Is Not One*, trans. C. Porter, Cornell UP, Ithaca, NY.

Jackson, David (1990) *Unmasking Masculinity: A Critical Autobiography*, Unwin Hyman, London.

Jardine, Alice (1987) 'Men in feminism: odor di uomo or compagnons de route' in Alice Jardine and Paul Smith, eds, *Men in Feminism*, Methuen, New York.

Jardine, Alice and Paul Smith (1987) *Men in Feminism*, Methuen, New York.

Kelly, Liz (1987) 'The continuum of sexual violence' in Jalna Hanmer and Mary Maynard, eds, *Women, Violence and Social Control*, Macmillan, London, 46–60.

Kimmel, Michael, ed. (1990a) 'After fifteen years: the impact of the sociology of masculinity on the masculinity of sociology' in Jeff Hearn and David H.J. Morgan, eds, *Men, Masculinities and Social Theory*, Unwin Hyman, London, 93–109.

Kinsman, Gary (1987) 'Gay macho' in Michael Kaufran, ed., *Beyond Patriarchy: Essays by Men on Power, Pleasure and Change*, Oxford University Press, Toronto, 103–19.

Knight, Chris (1989) *My Sex Life*, Women and Labour Collective, London.

Leclerc, Annie (1981) 'Woman's word' in Elaine Marks and Isabel de Courtivron, eds, *New French Feminisms*, Harvester, Brighton, 79–86.

Litewka, Jack (1977) 'The socialized penis' in Jon Snodgrass, ed., *A Book of Readings for Men Against Sexism*, Times Change, Albion, Ca., 16–35.

MacKinnon, Catharine (1982) 'Feminism, Marxism, method and the state: an agenda for theory,' *Signs*, 7(3), 634–58.

Mason, Steve (1986) 'Bristol men on the move,' *Men's Antisexist Newsletter*, 23.

Men, Masculinities and Socialism Group (1990) 'Changing men, changing politics,' *Achilles Heel* 10, 17–21.

Mercer, Kobena and Isaac Julien (1988) 'Race, sexual politics and black masculinity: a dossier' in Rowena Chapman and Jonathan Rutherford, eds, *Male Order: Unwrapping Masculinity*, Lawrence & Wishart, London, 97–164.

Metcalf, Andy and Martin Humphries, eds, (1985) *The Sexuality of Men*, Pluto, London.

Metcalf, Andy and Paul Morrison (1983) 'Sex in long-term relationships,' *Achilles Heel* 6 and 7, 19–21.

Morrison, Paul (1980) 'Our common ground . . .,' *Anti-Sexist Men's Newsletter*, 10.

Movement for a New Society (1977) *Gay Oppression and Liberation, Homophobia: Its Causes and Cure*, MNS, Philadelphia.

Moye, Andy (1985) 'Pornography' in Andy Metcalf and Martin Humphries, eds, *The Sexuality of Men*, Pluto, London, 44–69.

Redstockings Manifesto (1969) in Robin Morgan, ed., *Sisterhood is Powerful: An Anthology of Writings from the Women's Liberation Movement*, Vintage, New York, 598–601.

Rich, Adrienne (1980) 'Compulsory heterosexuality and lesbian existence,' *Signs*, 5(4), 631–60.

Rowan, John (1987) *The Horned God: Feminism and Men as Wounding and Healing*, Routledge, London.

Seidenberg, Robert (1970) *Marriage in Life and Literature*, Philosophical Library, New York.

Seidler, Victor J. (1987) 'Reason, desire and male sexuality' in Pat Caplan, *The Cultural Construction of Sexuality*, Tavistock, London, 82–112.

—— (1989) *Rediscovering Masculinity: Reason, Language and Sexuality*, Routledge, London.

Der Spiegel (1986) 'Schneller Schlag,' 17 February, 98–102.

Stanley, Liz (1984) 'Whales and minnows: some sexual theorists and their followers and how they contribute to making feminism invisible,' *Women's Studies International Forum*, 7(1), 53–62.

Stanley, Liz and Sue Wise (1983) *Breaking Out: Feminist Consciousness and Feminist Research*, Routledge, London.

Stoltenberg, John (1990a) 'Gays and the propornography movement: having the hots for sex discrimination' in Michael Kimmel, ed., *Men Confront Pornography*, Crown, New York, 248–62.

—— (1990b) *Refusing to be a Man*, Collins, London.

Stout, Ben (1984) 'From politically gay to publicly bisexual to personally celibate,' *Against Patriarchy*, 1, 1–20.

Tolson, Andrew (1977) *The Limits of Masculinity*, Tavistock, London.

Waring, Tony and Jim Wilson (1990) *Be Safe! A Self-Help Manual for Domestic Violence*, MOVE (Bolton), Bolton.

Wood, Robin (1987) 'Raging Bull: the homosexual subtext in film' in Michael Kaufman, ed., *Beyond Patriarchy: Essays by Men on Pleasure, Power and Change*, Oxford University Press, Toronto, 266–76.

Zita, Jacquelyn N. (1982) 'Historical amnesia and the lesbian continuum' in N.E. Keohane, M.Z. Rosaldo and B.C. Gelpi, eds, *Feminist Theory: A Critique of Ideology*, University of Chicago, Chicago, 161–76.

Index